The Universal Principles

of the

Reform Bahai Faith

by

Baha'u'llah

&

Abdu'l-Baha

Edited by Frederick Glaysher

Reform Bahai Press

Library of Congress Catalog card number:
2007942140

A full CIP record for this book is available from
the Library of Congress

2nd printing

Hardcover
ISBN-10: 0-9670421-3-5
ISBN-13: 978-09670421-3-8

Paper
ISBN-10: 0-9670421-0-0
ISBN-13: 978-09670421-0-7

Reform Bahai Press
P. O. Box 81842
Rochester, MI 48308 USA

O people of the world,
ye are all the fruit of one tree,
and the leaves of one branch.

Baha'u'llah

The Universal Principles
of the
Reform Bahai Faith

Contents

FOREWORD

The Universal Principles of the Bahai Movement, 1912

Through Baha'u'llah, his precursor the Bab, and Abdu'l-Baha, a universal religion has been given to the world. In their teachings the basic principles of all religions are demonstrated to be the same in kind and spirit, faith in the teachings of the past is strengthened and confirmed, and humanity finds the fatherhood of God and the brotherhood of man practically realized.

Many people are inquiring what new principles and teachings the Bahai Movement offers which are not already contained in the religions and philosophies of the past. Therefore it has seemed advisable to publish the accompanying compilation of excerpts from the writings of Baha'u'llah and Abdul-Baha in order to bring to the notice of the public some of the practical reforms and institutions for which their teaching stands. Like all the world's leaders of thought and morals the Bahai teachers have been far ahead of their time. A universal religion, international arbitration, universal peace, a universal language, universal suffrage and all of these reforms which compose a universal civilization, were unthought of by the world when, over half a century ago, these principles were first taught by the Bahais.

Those who wish to make a study of the Bahai Movement will find in its literature ample treatises through which the subject may also be approached from the spiritual and religious, as well as philosophic and prophetic viewpoints.

– Persian American Bulletin

INTRODUCTION

The universal teachings of Baha'u'llah and His son Abdu'l-Baha began in a world anything but universal. The Iran of 1844 was an isolated, backward, decadent kingdom, retrograde and oppressive in every way. Throughout their lives, Baha'u'llah and Abdu'l-Baha struggled to reform and reshape the spiritual and material resources of their homeland, until their focus enlarged from the provincial to the entire world. The forerunner of Baha'u'llah, the Bab, while shaking up a complacent Islam, was one more element they had to grow beyond. While much was left behind, they preserved in their spiritual teaching the essence of their religious heritage, while delivering God's new message for today, a modern message for all humankind, encircling the globe with a new prayer extolling the oneness of God, of humanity, and of all religions.

While the revelation of Baha'u'llah is voluminous, His vision is, like all great religions, a profoundly simple one of universal love and brotherhood, finding expression and practical effect in daily life, renewing the moral and spiritual fiber of the individual and the community, the experience and reality of worship and prayer, uplifting the human heart to new levels of possibility, service, and communion with God.

The Founder of the Bahai Faith believed in and taught a moderate, universal religion, grounded in a separation of church and state, not a theocracy, and members of the Reform Bahai Faith seek to recover and renew that saving vision for all humanity.

After a long flirtation with theocracy, many Bahais have awakened to the realization that a wrong turn was taken after the passing of Abdu'l-Baha in 1921. Though on a number of occasions Abdu'l-Baha had paradoxically taught "the Bahai Movement is not an organization" that did not prevent some Bahais from immediately setting out to organize it upon his death. The result has been a disappointing tale best told in the books of the early Reform Bahais Ruth White, Mirza Ahmad Sohrab, and Julie Chanler.

The newcomer to the Bahai Teachings will find here a brief but eloquent and inspiring introduction to the Faith of Baha'u'llah, while people already familiar with it will find a refreshing breeze has returned to revivify and uplift the spirit.

These selections will help the reader unfamiliar with the Bahai Teachings perceive and understand Baha'u'llah's vision, and will help people who accept Baha'u'llah as God's Messenger for today deepen their faith through study, meditation, and prayer.

This book marks the first publication of the Reform Bahai Press, which looks to more publications forthcoming.

Frederick Glaysher

Reform Bahai Faith
www.reformbahai.org

November 21, 2007

Baha'u'llah

Selections from the Writings of Baha'u'llah

I

It has been our aim to uplift men through exalted Words unto the Supreme Horizon and prepare them to hearken unto that which conduces to the sanctifying and purifying of the people of the world from the strife and discord resulting from differences in religions or sects.

O friends! In this day the Door of Heaven is opened by the key of the Godly Name, the Ocean of Generosity is manifested and is rolling before your faces, and the Sun of Providence is shining and gleaming; do not be exclusive, nor destroy your most precious time through the speech of this or that person. Gird up the loins of endeavor and do your best in training the people of the world. Do not imagine that the Cause of God is a cause of opposition, hatred and wrath. The Tongue of Greatness hath said that which is revealed from the Heaven of Will, in this Supreme Manifestation, is to unite the people with love and friendship toward all. The people of Baha who have drunk of the pure Wine of Reality must associate with all the world with the perfect spirit of joy and fragrance, and remind them of that which is for the benefit of all. This is the commandment of the Wronged One to His saints and sincere ones.

O people of the earth! Make not the religion of God a cause for variance among you. Verily, of a truth, it was revealed for the purpose of unifying the whole world. Blessed is he who loves the world simply for the sake of the Face of his Generous Lord.

We did not come except for the purpose of uniting whosoever is upon the earth and bringing them into perfect harmony and agreement.

II

With perfect compassion and mercy have we guided and directed the people of the world to that whereby their souls shall be profited. I declare by the Sun of Truth which hath shone forth from the highest horizons of the world that the people of Baha had not and have not any aim save the prosperity and reformation of the world and the purifying of the nations. With all men they have been in sincerity and charity.

III

Man should know his own self, and know those things which lead to loftiness or to baseness, to shame or to honor, to affluence or to poverty.

IV

In this Day the sun of arts and crafts is manifest from the horizon of the heaven of the Occident, and the river of skill is flowing from the sea of that region. One must speak with justice and recognize the worth of benefits. By the Life of God, the word Justice is shining and luminous like unto the sun.

V

Knowledge is like unto wings for the being of man, and is as a ladder for ascending. To acquire knowledge is incumbent on all, but of those sciences which may profit the people of the earth, and not such sciences as begin in mere words and end in mere words. The possessors of sciences and arts have a great right among the people of the world. Whereunto testifies the Mother of Divine Utterance in the Day of Return. Joy unto those who hear! Indeed the real treasury of man is his knowledge. Knowledge is the means of honor, prosperity, joy, gladness, happiness and exultation.

VI

It is made incumbent on every one of you to engage in some one occupation, such as arts, trades, and the like. We made this—your occupation—identical with the worship of God, the True One. Reflect, O people, upon the mercy of God upon His favors, then thank Him in mornings and evenings.

VII

Waste not your time in idleness and slothfulness, but occupy yourself with that whereby you will profit yourselves and others.

VIII

The most despised of men before God is he who sits and begs. Cling unto the rope of means, relying upon

God, the Causer of Causes. Every soul who occupies himself in an art or trade—this will be accounted an act of worship before God. Verily this is from no other than His great and abundant favor!

IX

Blessed are they who hold fast to the Rope of Compassion and Kindness and are detached from animosity and hatred.

X

The language of Love is the lodestone of hearts and the food of the soul; it stands in the relation of ideas to words and is an horizon for the shining of the Sun of Wisdom and Knowledge.

XI

This Oppressed One exhorts the people of the world to Forbearance and Benevolence. These are as two lights for the darkness of the world and as two teachers to lead nations to knowledge. Blessed are those who attain thereto, and woe unto those who are heedless.

XII

Good character is, verily, the best mantle for men on the part of God; by this God adorns the temples of His friends. By My Life the light of good character surpasses the light of the sun and its effulgence. He who attains thereto is accounted as the essence of men. Upon this the honor and glory of the world are based and are dependent. Good character is the means of guiding men to the Right Path and the Message.

XIII

Trustworthiness is the door of tranquility to all in the world, and the sign of glory from the presence of the Merciful One. Whosoever attains thereto has attained to treasuries of wealth and affluence. Trustworthiness is the greatest door to the security and tranquility of mankind. The stability of every affair always depends on it, and the worlds of honor, glory and affluence are illuminated by its light.

XIV

O friends of God, verily the Pen of Sincerity enjoineth on you the greatest faithfulness. By the Life of God, its light is more evident than the light of the sun! In its light and its brightness and its radiance every light is eclipsed. We desire of God that He will not withhold from His cities and lands the radiant effulgence of the sun of Faithfulness.

XV

Knowledge is one of the greatest benefits of God. To acquire knowledge is incumbent on all. These visible arts and present implements are from the results of His Knowledge and Wisdom, which have been revealed from

the Supreme Pen. In this Day the mysteries of this
earth unfolded and have become visible before the eyes.

XVI

O people of God! I exhort you to Reverence. Reverence
is, in the primary station, the lord of all virtues. Blessed
is he who is illumined with the light of Reverence, and
is adorned with the mantle of Uprightness! He who is
endowed with Reverence is endowed with a great
station.

XVII

Verily man becomes lofty through his trustworthiness,
chastity, judgment and virtues, and falleth through
treachery, folly and hypocrisy.

XVIII

Man must show forth fruits. A fruitless man, in the
words of His Holiness the Spirit (i. e., Christ), is like
unto a fruitless tree, and a fruitless tree is fit for fire.

XIX

O Son of Man! If thou lookest toward Mercy, regard not
that which benefits thee, and hold to that which will
benefit mankind: If thou lookest toward Justice, choose
thou for others what thou choosest for thyself. Verily,
through mercy man is elevated to the heaven of power;

and again, pride degrades him to the lowest station of humiliation and abasement.

XX

Charity is beloved and acceptable before God, and is accounted the chief among all good deeds. Consider, and then remember that which the Merciful One has revealed in the Qur'an: "But they prefer them the poor before themselves, although there be indigence among them. He who is preserved from the covetousness of his own soul, such shall surely prosper." Indeed, this blessed Word is, in this connection, a sun among words: Blessed is he who prefers his brother before himself; such an one is of the people of Baha!

XXI

O people of Baha! Ye are dawning-places of the Love and day-springs of the Favor of God. Defile not the tongues with cursing and execrating anyone and guard your eyes from that which is not worthy. Show forth that which ye possess, if it is accepted, the aim is attained; if not, interference is not allowable.

XXII

Fulfill the promise thou givest, and in all matters be just and equitable. Be silent among multitudes of men, and upright in giving decisions. Be humble toward men, be a lamp in darkness, a comforter in troubles, a sea to the thirsty, a refuge to the afflicted, a helper, assistant and succor to the oppressed.

XXIII

In actions and deeds be virtuous and pious. Be a home to the stranger, a healing to the sick, a stronghold to him who asks for help, a sight to the blind, a path to him who goeth astray. Be thou the beauty of the face of truth, an adornment to the temple of faithfulness, a throne to the house of character, a spirit to the body of the world, a banner to the hosts of justice and a light to the horizon of goodness.

Be thou a dew to the fertile and rich ground, an ark to the sea of science, a star in the heaven of generosity, a diadem to the head of wisdom, a white spot on the forehead of time, and a fruit of the tree of humbleness.

Be patient in misfortunes and contented in all aspects. In truth be firm and unwavering; be quick in doing good deeds; be assiduous toward God; be a veiler of people's faults; be an avoider of lust. Be a runner after the truth; a cloud of bounty to the servants of God; be kindly to thy debtors; be a forgiver to the transgressors; be a fulfiller of the Covenant and steadfast in the Cause.

XXIV

Everyone who desireth victory must first subdue the city of his own heart with the sword of spiritual truth and of the Word, and must protect it from remembering aught besides God; afterwards let him turn his regards towards the cities of others' hearts. This is what is meant by "victory!"

XXV

It is forbidden to drink that which will destroy the mind. Every rational being should do that which befitteth a man, not that which is practiced by the careless and heedless.

XXVI

Well is it with him who is adorned with the decoration of manners and morals; verily he is of those who help their Lord with clear perspicuous action.

XXVII

Gambling and the use of opium are strictly prohibited. Beware not to practice that which will enfeeble your temples and harm your bodies.

XXVIII

Among the people are those who glory in a desire for liberty. Know that the animal is the symbol of liberty and manifestation thereof, hence it behooveth man to put himself under laws which will protect him against the ignorance of himself, and the injury of the deceitful. Liberty is confined to compliance with the Commandments of God. If ye adopt that which He hath revealed for you from the Heaven of Inspiration, ye will find yourselves in perfect and pure freedom. The liberty which profits you is that which is confined to your servitude to God, the Truth. He who tastes its sweetness will never exchange it for the possessions of the realms of the heavens and earths.

XXIX

Consort with the people of religions with joy and fragrance. The followers of Sincerity and Faithfulness must consort with all the people of the world with joy and fragrance; for association is always conducive to union and harmony, and union and harmony are the cause of the order of the world and the life of nations.

XXX

The Fire of Love will assemble all the different people in one court; but the fire of animosity is the cause of disunion and conflict.

XXXI

It is sanctioned that all the nations of the world consort with each other with joy and fragrance. Consort ye, O people, with the people of all religions with joy and fragrance. We have said—and our saying is truth—Consort with all the people of religions with joy and fragrance. Through this Utterance whatever was the cause of foreignness, discord and disunion has been removed.

XXXII

All must adhere to the means which is conducive to Love and Unity.

XXXIII

O people of the world, ye are all the fruit of one tree, and the leaves of one branch. Walk with perfect charity, concord, affection and agreement. I declare by the Sun of Truth, the light of agreement shall brighten and illumine all the horizons.

XXXIV

You must show forth that which will be conducive to the welfare and tranquility of the helpless ones of the world. Gird up the loins of effort; perchance the slaves may be emancipated from bondage and find freedom.

XXXV

It is revealed in one of the Tablets: "O people of God! Be not occupied with yourselves. Be intent on the betterment of the world and the training of nations." The betterment of the world can be accomplished through pure and excellent deeds and well-approved and agreeable conduct. The helper of the Cause is Deeds and its assistant is Good Character.

XXXVI

It behooveth the people of Baha to assist the Lord through their utterance and to preach unto the world through their deeds and good morals. The effect of deeds is greater than the effect of words.

XXXVII

In former ages it has been said: "To love one's native land is Faith." But the tongue of Grandeur hath said in the Day of this Manifestation: "Glory is not his who loves his native land; but glory is his who loves his kind." By these exalted Words He taught the birds of souls a new flight and effaced restriction and blind imitation from the Book.

XXXVIII

The most splendid fruit of the Tree of Knowledge is this exalted Word: Ye are all fruits of one tree and leaves of one branch.

XXXIX

Be generous when in affluence and grateful when thou art poor. Be faithful to the rights of others. Let thy face be bright and open and be a treasure to the poor and needy. Be an admonisher to the rich, and an answerer to those who call on thee.

XL

O children of dust, let the rich learn the midnight sighing of the poor, lest negligence destroy them and they be deprived of their portion of the tree of wealth. O ye who are wealthy on earth, the poor among ye are my trust, therefore guard my trust, and be not wholly occupied with your own ease.

XLI

O ye rich people! When ye see a poor man do not grow proud and haughty and despise him, but think from what ye were created. Do ye imagine that ye will be profited by what ye have? It will be possessed by some one in your stead, and ye shall return to the dust without finding any one to succor or help. Of what use is a life that is ruled by death, or a duration which vanisheth, or a grace that changeth?

XLII

In this Day, it is incumbent and obligatory upon all to adhere to that which is conducive to the progress and elevation of the just government and people.

XLIII

This Oppressed One hath loved and loves the philosophers, that is—those whose philosophy hath not been mere words, but who have produced lasting results and fruits in the world. To respect these blessed souls is incumbent on all. Blessed are those who practice.

XLIV

O ye wise men among nations! Turn your eyes from foreignness and gaze unto Oneness, and hold fast unto the means which conduce to the tranquility and security of the people of the whole world. This span-wide world is but one land and one locality. Abandon that glory which is the cause of discord and turn unto that which promotes harmony. To the people of Baha glory is in knowledge, good deeds, good morals and wisdom, not in native land or station. O people of the earth, appreciate the worth of this Heavenly Word; for it is like unto a ship for the sea of Knowledge, and is as the sun to the universe of Perception.

XLV

In every country or government where any of this community reside, they must behave toward that with faithfulness, trustfulness and truthfulness.

XLVI

O people of the Earth! A solitary life and severe discipline do not meet God's approval. The possessors of perception and knowledge should look unto the means which are conducive to joy and fragrance. Such practices come forth and proceed from the loins of superstition and the womb of fancy, and are not worthy of the people of knowledge. Some of the people of the past and of later times dwelt in mountain and caves, and others frequented the tombs during the night. Hearken to the advice of this Oppressed One. Abandon that which ye hold, and adhere unto what the Trustworthy Counselor commands. Deprive not yourselves of that which is created for you.

XLVII

The sinner, when in a state wherein he finds himself free and severed from all else save God, must beg for

God's forgiveness and pardon. At the same time such confession before men leads to one's humiliation and abasement, and God—Exalted in His Glory!—does not wish for the humiliation of his servants. Verily He is Compassionate and Beneficent.

A sinner must privately, between himself and God, beg for mercy from the Sea of Mercy and ask forgiveness from the Heaven of Beneficence.

XLVIII

The pious practices of the monks and priests among the people of His Holiness the Spirit (Christ)—upon Him is the Peace of God and His Glory!—are remembered before God; but, in this day they must abandon solitude for open places, and engage in that which may profit both themselves and other men. We have conferred permission on them all to engage in matrimony, so that there may appear from them those who may celebrate the praise of God, the Lord of the Seen and Unseen and the Lord of the Lofty Throne.

XLIX

Gaze toward the horizon of Justice and Equity under all circumstances. This exalted Utterance has been revealed, from the Pen of Abha in the *Hidden Words*.

"O Son of Spirit!

"The best of all to Me is Justice. Desire thou not to cast it away if thou desirest Me and neglect it not, that thou may'st be faithful to Me, for by it thou wilt attain to see things with thine own eyes and not by the eyes of the creatures and know them by thine own knowledge and not by the knowledge of any in the world. Meditate on this—how thou oughtest to be. Justice is one of My Gifts to thee and one of My Cares over thee, therefore put it before thine eyes continually."

The possessors of Justice and Equity occupy the highest station and loftiest rank; the lights of Righteousness and Piety radiate and shine from such souls. It is hoped that nations and countries may not be deprived of the lights of these two orbs.

The light of men is Justice; quench it not with the contrary winds of oppression and tyranny. The purpose of justice is the appearance of unity among people. In this exalted Word, the sea of God's wisdom is moving. All the books of the world are not sufficient to contain its interpretation.

L

God has imposed on every town erection of a House of Justice where men are to assemble according to the number of Baha (if they surpass this number it matters little). They should figure to themselves that they are in God's presence, and see what is invisible. They should be divine agents in the causal world, the representatives of God for those who are on earth, and defend for love of God the interests of His servants as they would defend their own.

The Members of the House of Justice of God must, night and day, gaze toward that which hath been revealed from the horizon of the Heaven of the Supreme Pen for the training of the servants, for the upbuilding of countries, for the protection of men and for the preservation of human honor.

LI

We exhort the members of the House Justice, and command them to guard and protect the servants, maidservants and children.

LII

The affairs of the people are in charge of the members of the House of Justice. They are the trustees of God among His servants and the sources of command in his countries.

LIII

It is decreed that every father must educate his sons and daughters in learning and in writing and also in that which hath been ordained in the Tablet. He who neglects that which hath been commanded in this matter, if he is rich, it is incumbent on the trustees of the House of Justice to recover from him the amount required for the education of the children; otherwise, if the parent is not capable, the matter shall devolve on the House of Justice. Verily We have made the House of Justice an asylum for the poor and needy.

He who educates his son, or any other's children, it is as though he hath educated one of My children. Upon such an one be Baha, My Providence and My Mercy, which hath embraced all in the world!

LIV

Men and women must place a part of what they earn

31

by trade, agriculture, or other business, in charge of a trustworthy person, to be spent in the education and instruction of the children. That deposit must be invested in the education of the children, under the advice of the Trustees or members of the House of Justice.

LV

We desire but the good of the world and the happiness of the nations. That all nations should become one in faith and all men as brothers; that the bonds of affection and unity between the sons of men should be strengthened; that diversity of religion should cease, and differences of race be annulled—what harm is there in this? Yet so it shall be; these fruitless strifes, these ruinous wars shall pass away, and the "Most Great Peace" shall come. Do not you in Europe need this also? Is not this that which Christ foretold? Yet do we see your kings and rulers lavishing their treasures more freely on means for the destruction of the human race than on that which would conduce to the happiness of mankind. These strifes and this bloodshed and discord must cease, and all men be as one kindred and one family. Let not a man glory in this, that he loves his country; let him rather in this, that he loves his kind.

LVI

We ask God that He will help the Kings to be at peace; verily He is able to do what He willeth. O assembly of Kings! Verily we see you increasing your expenditure every year, and placing the burden thereof on your subjects; this is nought but manifest injustice. Fear ye the sighs of the oppressed and his tears, and do not burden your subjects above that which they can bear, neither ruin them to build up your palaces. Choose for them that which ye choose for yourselves; thus do we expound unto you that which will profit you, if ye are of those who enquire.

LVII

The Members of the House of Justice must promote the Most Great Peace, in order that the world may be free from onerous expenditures. This matter is obligatory and indispensable; for warfare and conflict are the foundation of trouble and distress.

LVIII

We have commanded the Most Great Peace, which is the greatest means for the protection of mankind. The rulers of the world must, in one accord, adhere to this Command, which is the main cause for the security and tranquility of the world. We beg of God to assist them in that which is conducive to the peace of the people.

LIX

The Third Glad Tidings is the study of various languages. This command hath formerly flowed from the Supreme Pen. Their Majesties, the Kings—may God assist them—or the Counselors of the earth must consult together, and appoint one of the existing languages or a new language, and instruct the children therein, in all the schools of the world; and the same must be done in respect to writing also. In such case the earth will be considered as one.

LX

The Sixth Ishraq is concerning union and harmony among mankind. Through union the regions of the world have been illuminated with the light of the Cause. The greatest means for this end is that the peoples should be familiar with each other's writing and language.

LXI

At this moment the Supreme Pen exhorts the daysprings of power and dawning-places of authority, to wit: kings, rulers, chiefs, princes, learned men of religion and mystics, and commands them to hold fast to Religion. Religion is the greatest instrument for the order of the world and the tranquility of all existent beings. The weakness of the pillars of Religion has encouraged the ignorant and rendered them audacious and arrogant. Truly, I say, whatever lowers the lofty station of religion will increase heedlessness in the wicked, and finally result in anarchy. Hear, O ye who are endowed with sight!

LXII

The people of wealth and men of honor and power must have the best possible regard and respect for Religion. Religion is a manifest light and a strong fortress for the protection and tranquility of the people of the world. For the fear of God commands people to do that which is just and forbids them that which is evil. If the lamp of Religion remain concealed, agitation and anarchy would prevail, and the orb of Justice and Equity and the sun of Peace and Tranquility would be withheld from giving light.

LXIII

The religion of God and the Creed of God hath been revealed and made manifest from the heaven of the Will of the King of Pre-existence for the sake of union and harmony among the people of the world; make it not a means for disagreement and discord.

LXIV

The First Glad Tidings which is conferred in this Most Great Manifestation on all the people of the world, from the "Mother Book," is the abolishing of the decree of religious warfare from the Book.

LXV

O unitarians, make firm the girdle of endeavor, that perchance religious strife and conflict may be removed from amongst the people of the world and be annulled. For love of God and His servants engage in this great and mighty matter. Religious hatred and rancor is a world-consuming fire, and the quenching thereof most arduous, unless the hand of Divine Might give men deliverance from this unfruitful calamity. Consider a war which happeneth between two states: both sides have foregone wealth and life; how many villages were beheld as though they were not! This precept is in the position of the light in the lamp of utterance.

LXVI

O people of God!—Exalted in His Glory!—Ask God to guard the sources of power and authority against the evil of egotism and lust and to illumine them with the lights of justice and guidance.

LXVII

A king whom the pride of authority and independence does not withhold from being just, and whom benefits, opulence, glory, hosts and legions do not deprive of the splendors of the Orb of Equity—such a king shall possess a lofty station and an exalted rank in the Supreme Concourse; it is incumbent on all to assist and love such a blessed being. Blessed is the ruler, who controls the reins of the ego, and overcomes his wrath; who prefers justice to oppression and equity to tyranny!

LXVIII

We ask the manifestation of Power, that is, kings and leaders, to endeavor, perchance discord may vanish and the world be illumined with the light of accord.

LXIX

The Third Ishraq commands the executing of the penal laws, for this is the primary means for the maintenance of the world. The heaven of Divine Wisdom is illumined and shining with two orbs—Consultation and Kindness. And the tent of the order of the world is hoisted and established on two pillars, Reward and Retribution.

LXX

Governments must be acquainted with the conditions or deserts of the officials and must confer upon them dignity and positions in accord with their due measure and merit. To have regard for this matter is obligatory and incumbent on every chief and ruler. Thus, perchance, traitors shall not usurp the place of trustworthy men, or spoilers occupy the seat of guardians.

LXXI

Complete regard should be had to the matter of agriculture. This matter is in reality endowed with the first station.

LXXII

The deniers and contradictors hold to four words:

First: Destroying men's lives.
Second: Burning the books.

Third : Shunning other nations.

Fourth: Exterminating other nations.

Now, by the Grace and Authority of the Word of God, these four great barriers have been demolished. These four manifest decrees have been effaced from the Book, and God hath changed brutal manners into spiritual qualities.

LXXIII

O ye people of the world! The virtue of this Most Great Manifestation is that We have effaced from the Book whatever was the cause of difference, corruption and discord, and recorded therein that which leads to Unity, Harmony and Accord.

LXXIV

Strife and contest were and are seemly in the beasts of prey, but laudable actions are seemly in man.

LXXV

The pages of swiftly appearing newspapers are indeed the mirror of the world; they display the doings and actions of the different nations; they both illustrate them and cause them to be heard. Newspapers are as a mirror which is endowed with hearing, sight and speech; they are a wonderful phenomenon and a great matter. But it behooveth the writers thereof to be sanctified from the prejudice of egotism and desire and to be adorned with the ornament of Equity and Justice; they must inquire into matters as much as possible in order that they may be informed of the real facts and commit the same to writing.

LXXVI

Proclaim: Verily the Mashriqu'l-Adhkar will be a House built in my name in every country and city. Verily we have called it by that name, were you of those who know.

Spirit of the Age

Baha'u'llah

Whosoever wisheth, let him advance, and whosoever wisheth, let him deny; verily God is independent of him and of that which he may see and witness.

God, singly and alone, abideth in His Place which is Holy above space and time, mention and utterance, sign, description and definition, height and depth.

God hath been and is everlastingly hidden in His Own Essence and will be eternally concealed from eyes and sight in His Identity. Nay, there hath not ever been nor will be any connection or relation between the created beings and His word. Therefore God caused brilliant Essences of Sanctity to appear from the holy worlds of the Spirit, in human bodies, walking among mankind; in accordance with His abundant mercy. These Mirrors of Sanctity fully express that Sun of Existence and Essence of Desire. Their knowledge expresses His knowledge, their power His power, their dominion His dominion, their beauty His beauty, and their manifestation His Manifestation. Therefore whosoever is favored by these shining and glorious lights and hath attained to these luminous, radiant Suns of Truth during every Manifestation, hath attained the Meeting of God, and entered the city of eternal life. This station is assigned only to His Prophets and Holy Ones, because no greater and mightier than they have appeared in the realm of existence. Consequently, by meeting these Holy Lights, the "Meeting of God" is attained; through their Knowledge, the Knowledge of God, and by their Countenance the Countenance of God. This Meeting can never be realized by any except in the Resurrection Day, which is the Self of God arisen in His Universal Manifestation.

O God! This is a Day the Light of which Thou hast sanctified above the sun and its effulgence. I testify that this Day is illumined by the Light of Thy Countenance and by the effulgence of the dawning Lights of Thy Manifestation.

O Thou, my God, and the Beloved of my heart! With the name of this Day Thou hast adorned Thy Tablet, which is known only to Thee. Thou hast called it " The Day of God." Nothing is to be seen therein but Thy Supreme Self, and naught is to be remembered save Thy sweetest Name.

The Day of the Return to God hath come; arise from your seats, and praise and glorify your Lord, the Omniscient, the Wise. He who findeth Life in this Day shall never die, and he who dieth in this Day, shall never find Life.

This is the meaning of that "resurrection" recorded in all the Books, and which Day hath been announced to all. Consider, is there any day to be imagined greater, mightier and more excellent than this Day, that man should turn away from it and deprive himself of its bounties, pouring like the spring rain from the presence of the Merciful?

O my brother, understand then the meaning of resurrection, and purify thine ears from the sayings of rejected people. Shouldst thou step a little way into the worlds of Severance, thou wilt testify that no day greater than this Day, and no resurrection mightier than this Resurrection can be imagined, and that one deed in this Day is equivalent to deeds performed during a hundred thousand years.

The Pillar of God is being erected and hath become manifest by His providence and command. The time of

41

former things is past and a new time has been produced, and all things are made new by the desire of God. But only a new eye can perceive and a new mind can comprehend this Station. The Beginning and the End bore allusion to One Blessed Word, and that hath come and is manifest. That Word is the Soul of the Divine Books and Epistles, which hath forever been and will be forevermore. That Word is the key to the Most Great Divine Treasure and to the Supreme Hidden Mystery which hath ever been concealed behind the veil of preservation. That Word is the same Alpha and Omega prophesied of by John. Verily He is the First and the Last, the Manifest and the Hidden.

Although the purpose of learning is the attainment and knowledge of this station, yet all are occupied with outward learnings and desist from them not even for a moment; closing their eyes to the essence of Knowledge and the knowable. It seems as if they had not drunk one drop from the ocean of Divine Knowledge nor attained a sprinkling of the cloud of the Merciful Bounty. But We have consumed the greatest veil, with the saying: "Knowledge is the greatest veil."

But O my brother, when a seeker intends to turn the step of search and journeying into the path of the Knowledge of the King of Pre-existence, he must first cleanse and purify his heart—which is the place of the appearance and emanation of the splendor of the hidden mysteries of Divinity, and he must cleanse and refine his breast—which is the throne for the accession and establishment of the love of the Eternal Beloved—from the gloomy dusts of acquired learning and from the allusions of satanic appearances. He must likewise sanctify his heart from attachment to water and clay—in such manner that no trace of love or hatred may remain in the heart, lest that love may cause him to incline toward a direction without guide, or that

42

hatred prevent him from the direction of reality. He should at all times trust in God, and turn away from the creatures; be severed and detached from the world of dust and united with the Lord of Lords.

When the lamp of search, effort, longing, fervor, love, rapture, attraction and devotion is enkindled in the heart, and the breeze of love blows forth from the direction of Unity, the darkness of error, doubt and uncertainty will be dispelled and the lights of Knowledge and Assurance will encompass all the pillars of existence. Then the ideal Herald will dawn as the true morn from the Divine City, with spiritual glad tidings, and awaken the heart, soul and spirit from the sleep of negligence, with the trumpet of Knowledge. Then the favors and confirmations of the eternal Holy Spirit will impart such a new life that one will find himself the possessor of a new eye, a new ear, a new heart, and a new mind, and will direct his attention to the clear, universal signs and to the hidden individual secrets. With the new eye of God he will see a door open in every atom for attainment to the stations of positive Knowledge, certain Truth, and evident Light; and will perceive in all things the mysteries of the splendor of Oneness and the traces of the Manifestation of Eternity.

What shall we mention of the signs, tokens, appearances and splendors ordained in that Divine City, by the command of the King of Names and Attributes! The mystery of the fire of Moses is revealed in its wonderful tulips, and the breath of the Holy Spirit of Jesus emanates from its fragrances of holiness. It bestows wealth without gold and grants immortality without death. Those who earnestly endeavor in the way of God, after severance from all else, will become so attached to that City that they will not abandon it for an instant. This City is the Revelation of God, renewed every one thousand years, more or less. For instance, in the age of Moses, it was the Pentatuch; in the time of Jesus, the Gospel; in the day of Mohamet the Messenger of God, the Qur'an; and in the Day of Him whom God shall send forth, His Book, which is the return of all the books and their Guardian.

Consider how great is the value and how paramount the importance of the Revelations in which God hath completed His perfect argument, consummate proof, dominant power and penetrating will. To the people they are everlasting proof, fixed argument and shining light from the presence of that Ideal King. No excellence equals them and nothing precedes them. They are the firm thread, the strong rope, the most secure handle and the inextinguishable light. Through them flows the river of the Divine Knowledge, and bursts the fire of the consummate Wisdom of the Eternal. This is a fire from which two effects proceed at the same time: it creates the heat of love within the people of faith, and produces the cold of heedlessness within the people of hatred. The proof of the sun is its light which shines forth and encompasses the world; and the argument of the shower is its bounty which renews the world with a fresh mantle. Yea! The blind realize no effect in the sun but heat, and a barren soil knoweth no bounty from the vernal mercy.

Dost thou think thy body a small thing when within it is enclosed the universe?

Cleanse the people with the water of the inner significances which We have deposited in the signs. By My Life, it is indeed the Water of Life which the Merciful One hath sent down from the Heaven of Grace for the life of the people of the world!

I testify that verily there is no God save He! and He who hath come is verily the Hidden Mystery, the Concealed Secret, the Most Great Book for the nations, and the Heaven of Beneficence to the world. He is the

Mighty Sign among mankind, and the Dawning Place of the Highest Attributes in the world of emanation. Through Him hath appeared that which was concealed from all eternity and was hidden from men of discernment, Verily, He is the One whose Manifestation was announced by the Books of God in former and latter times. Whosoever acknowledges Him, His signs and His evidences hath verily acknowledged that which the Tongue of Grandeur hath uttered before the creation of heaven and earth, and before the appearance of the Kingdom of Names. Through Him the sea of knowledge hath moved among mankind, and the running water of Wisdom hath flowed from God, the King of Days. Joy unto him who, in this Day, casts away that which is possessed by the people, and holds fast to that which is commanded on the part of God, the King of Names and the Creator.

This world is a show without reality, and is a non-existence adorned in the form of existence. Do not attach your hearts thereto. Do not sever yourselves from the Creator, and be not of those who are heedless!

Seeking to know your own selves, which is identical with knowing Myself, you will become independent of all save Me, and you will see the Ocean of My Providence and the Deep of My Beneficence in yourselves with the outward and inward eye as manifest and clear as the sun shining from the Name of Abha. All things are a proof of your existence, if ye emerge from the gloomy dust of non-existence. Be not grieved at the hardships of these numbered days; for every destruction is followed by a construction, and a Paradise of Rest is concealed in every hardship.

Consider the people, their states and conditions! They have been anxiously awaiting, days and nights, for the One whom they were promised in the Book of God; but when the exact time had come, and the banner of the

45

Appearance grew manifest, they turned away from God, the Mighty, the Exalted. But we announce to thee the good news of the appearance of God, of His Dominion, Might and Potency, that thou mayest rejoice and be of the thankful. Beware not to let the affairs of men trouble thee, nor the illusions of those who have rejected, as a falsehood to frighten thee, the belief of the Origin and Return. Thou art from God, and unto God shalt thou return!

O Son of Spirit! I have created thee rich. Why dost thou make thyself poor? Noble have I made thee. Why dost thou degrade thyself? Of the essence of Knowledge have I manifested thee. Why searchest for another than Me? From the clay of Love I have kneaded thee. Why seekest thou another? Turn thy sight unto thyself, that thou mayest find Me standing within thee, Powerful, Mighty and Supreme.

Oh ye people of the world! The virtue of this Most Great Manifestation is that We have removed from the Book whatever was the cause of difference, corruption and discord, and recorded therein that which leads to unity, harmony and agreement. God manifested Himself to teach the people the truth, sincerity, religion, faith, submission, reconciliation, compassion, courtesy, piety; and to teach them how to adorn themselves with the garments of good qualities and holy deeds.

Be a lamp in darkness, a comforter in troubles, a sea to the thirsty, a refuge to the afflicted, a helper, an assistant and a succor to the oppressed. In actions and deeds be virtuous and pious. To the stranger be a home; to the sick a remedy; to him who asks for help a stronghold; to the blind be sight; to him who goes astray a pathway; to the face of truth, beauty; to the temple of faithfulness an embroidered garment; to the house of characters and manners a throne; to the body of the world a spirit; to the hosts of justice a banner; to the horizon of good a light; to the fertile and rich ground, dew; to the sea of science an ark; to the heaven of generosity a star; to the head of wisdom a diadem; to the forehead of time a white light; and to the tree of humility, fruitfulness.

This is that matter which shall never change. Know that in every age and dispensation all divine ordinances are changed, according to the requirements of the time, except the law of Love which, like unto a fountain, flows always and is never overtaken by change.

Render God victorious by wisdom. Glory be upon the people of Glory!

Hidden Words

From the Arabic of Baha'u'llah

Of the Utterances which descended from the Majestic Might through the tongue of Power and Strength on the prophets of the past, we have taken the essence and in the garment of Brevity clothed it. And this is a kindness to the Beloved, that they may be enabled to fulfil the Covenant of God and to perform in themselves that which He has entrusted to them, that through the excellence of devotion, which is of the Spirit, they may win the Victory.

1. O Son of Spirit!
The first Utterance declareth: Possess a good, pure, and enlightened heart, for therein is the Kingdom, Eternal, Unpassing, Ancient.

2. O Son of Spirit!
The best of all to Me is Justice. Cast it not aside if thou desirest Me. Neglect it not. By it thou wilt be strengthened to see all things, not with the eyes of men, but with thine own, to know all things, not by the knowledge of any in the world, but of thyself. Upon this meditate—how thou oughtest to be. The power of discernment have I given thee. This is My Providence for thee; keep it ever before thine eyes.

3. O Son of Man!
I was in My Ancient Essence and My Everlasting Being. I foreknew My Love for thee; therefore I created thee and laid upon thee My Likeness and manifested in thee My Beauty.

4. O Son of Man!

Because thy creation rejoiced Me, therefore I created thee. Love Me, that I may acknowledge thee and in the Spirit of Life confirm thee.

5. O Son of Existence!

Love Me, that thou mayest know My Love for thee. If thou lovest Me not, My Love can never reach thee. Know this, O Servant!

6. O Son of Existence!

Thy rose-garden is My Love, thy paradise is My Nearness. Therefore enter in and tarry not. In My Supreme Majesty, in My Highest Kingdom, it is this which has been ordained for thee.

7. O Son of Humanity!

If thou desirest Me, love not thyself. If thou seekest My Grace, value not thine own. Thus thou wilt be transient in Me, but in thee I will be everlasting.

8. O Son of Spirit!

For thee no peace has been ordained save by turning from thyself and advancing towards Me. Verily it is the Law that thy glory is in My Name and not in thine own; that thy dependence is on My countenance and not on thine. For verily I am to be beloved above all that is.

9. O Son of Existence!

My Love is My Kingdom. Whosoever enters it is safe; whoever seeks it not is led astray and perishes.

10. O Son of Truth!

Of My Kingdom art thou; come into it, that thou mayest attain to Eternal Truth. My Love is in thee; know it to be thyself, that thou mayest find Me near.

11. O Son of Existence!
My Vase thou art; My Light is in thee. Be enlightened
by it and seek not any besides Me; for I have made thee
rich and abundantly bestowed My Grace upon thee.

12. O Son of Existence!
By the Hand of Power I made thee, by the Fingers of
Strength I created thee, and in thee I placed the essence
of My Light. Therefore depend upon this and upon
naught else; for verily Mine Action is perfect and My
Decree shall prevail. Doubt not this, question it not.

13. O Son of Spirit!
I created thee rich. How is it that thou makest thyself
poor? I made thee mighty. How is it that thou holdest
thyself cheap? From the essence of Knowledge I brought
thee forth. How is it that thou seekest aught besides
Me? From the clay of Love I kneaded thee. How is it
that thou turnest from Me? Direct thy sight to thine own
being, that thou mayest find Me standing in thee,
Powerful, Mighty, Supreme.

14. O Son of Man!
Thou art My Possession, and My Possession will never
be destroyed. How is it that thou fearest thy
destruction? Thou art My Light, and My Light will
never be extinguished. How is it that thou apprehendest
thy extinction? Thou art My Garment, and My Garment
will never be worn out. Therefore rest thou in thy love
for Me, that thou mayest find Me in the
Highest Horizon.

15. O Son of Truth!
Turn to My Face and withdraw from all else besides
Me; for verily Mine Authority is enduring and will never
end, My Kingdom is eternal and will never be

overthrown. If thou seekest something besides Me, thou wilt find it not—yea, even though thou searchest the universe for ever and ever.

16. O Son of Light!
Forget all else in Me, be comforted by My Spirit. This is the essence of My Command; therefore abide in it steadfastly.

17. O Son of Man!
Let thy satisfaction be in Me—not in the things of the world. Seek no refuge besides Me; for verily there is naught else that will ever satisfy thee.

18. O Son of Spirit!
Ask thou not of Me that which I desire not for thee. Be thou satisfied with what I have ordained to thy countenance; for that will benefit thee—if with it thou art content.

19. O Son of Divine Wisdom!
I placed in thee a spirit from Me that thou mightest be My Lover. Why hast thou left Me and sought another lover?

20. O Son of Spirit!
My Right to thee is great and cannot be denied; My Bounty to thee is ample, and cannot be ignored; My Love for thee is real and cannot be forgotten; My Light for thee is shining and cannot be concealed.

21. O Son of Humanity!
I have ordained for thee from the Tree of Wisdom the Holiest Fruits. How is it that thou hast turned from them and been content with what is common? Return thou to thy heritage in the Highest Horizon.

22. O Son of Spirit!

I created thee sublime, but thou hast made thyself ordinary. Ascend to that for which thou wert created.

23. O Son of the Unseen Supreme Kingdom!

I beckoned thee to life, but thou preferrest death. Wherefore hast thou turned from My desire and followed thine own will?

24. O Son of Man!

Transgress not the bounds of thy limitation, claim not for thyself what thou shouldst not claim. Adore the Countenance of thy Lord, the Mighty, the Powerful.

25. O Son of Spirit!

Dost thou boast thyself over the poor? Verily I walk before them; and I behold thee in thy miserable state and for ever grieve for thee.

26. O Son of Existence!

How is it that thou hast forgotten thine own faults, and occupiest thyself with the shortcomings of My People? In that thou doest thus thou condemnest thyself.

27. O Son of Man!

So long as thou thyself sinnest, breathe not of the sins of any. If thou violatest this command, of the earth art thou. To this I bear witness.

28. O Son of Spirit!

Lay not upon any man what thou wouldest not have placed against thyself, and promise not what thou wilt not fulfil. This is My Command to thee; obey it.

29. O Son of Spirit!

Know verily that he who exhorts men to equity and

himself does iniquity is not of Me, though he bear My name.

30. O Son of Man!

Hinder not My servant in whatsoever he may ask of thee; for his face is My Face, and Me thou must revere.

31. O Son of Existence!

Ponder well thy deeds each day, as though thou wert to be judged for them; for verily death cometh to thee, and then thy deeds will judge thee.

32. O Son of the Unseen Spiritual Kingdom!

I made death as glad tidings for thee. How is it that thou despairest at its approach? I gave thee enlightenment to guide thee. How is it that thou veilest thyself from it ?

33. O Son of Spirit!

The Gospel of Light I herald to thee; gladden thyself with it. To the State of Holiness I call thee; enter its shelter that thou mayest rest for ever.

34. O Son of Spirit!

The Holy Spirit heralds comfort to thee. How is it that thou art sorrowful? The Spirit of Command confirms thee in the Cause. How is it that thou tarriest? The light of My countenance shines before thee. How is it that thou goest astray?

35. O Son of Man!

Be not sorrowful save when thou art far from Me; be not happy save when thou art returning to Me, when thou art near Me.

36. O Son of Man!

Cheer thy heart with delight, that thou mayest be fitted to meet Me and become a mirror of My Splendour.

37. O Son of Man!

Clothe thy nakedness with the Splendour of My Garment. Deprive thyself not of thy portion of My Beautiful Fountains, lest thirst possess thee for ever.

38. O Son of Existence!

Keep My Commands because thou lovest Me. Cut thyself off from thine own desires, if thou seekest My Pleasure.

39. O Son of Man!

Neglect not My Laws, if thou lovest My Beauty; forget not My Commandments, if thou desirest My Blessing.

40. O Son of Man!

Speed thee to the land of the Supreme Kingdom, haste to the space of Heaven. Thou wilt not find rest save in obedience to My Command and in devotion before My Face.

41. O Son of Man!

Glorify My Cause, that I may make known to thee the secrets of My Greatness and shine upon thee with the Enlightenment which is eternal.

42. O Son of Man!

Obey Me that I may come to thee. Advance My Cause that thou mayest be crowned a Victor in the Kingdom.

43. O Son of Existence!

Mention Me in Mine Earth that I may mention thee in My Heaven; that thine eye and Mine Eye may be content.

44. O Son of the Throne!

Thy hearing is My Hearing; hear thou with it. Thy sight is My Sight; see thou with it. Attest for Me in thine inmost soul a supreme holiness, that I may attest for thee in Myself an exalted place.

45. O Son of Existence!

Suffer in My Cause with a joyful heart, receive with thankfulness that which I have destined for thee; that thou mayest rest with Me in the tents of Glory behind the veils of Might.

46. O Son of Man!

Consider what it behooves thee to do; act wisely. Is it dearer to thee to die upon thy bed, or to be martyred in My Name upon the dust and become the Dawning- place of My Cause and the Manifestation of My Light in the highest estate of Paradise? Be wise, O Servant!

47. O Son of Man!

By my Splendour! Thy will to tinge thy hair with thy blood is dearer to Me than the two realms of the universe, than the brilliance of the two Great Lights. Therefore cherish it, O Servant!

48. O Son of Man!

To everything there is a sign; and the sign of Love is patience to endure the trials, the destiny, ordained by Me.

49. O Son of Man!

The true lover longs for the test as the rebel for pardon, as the criminal for mercy.

50. O Son of Man!

If thou avoidest affliction how canst thou walk in the hard way of those who are content with that which pleaseth Me? If thou fearest lest calamity befall thee on My Path, how canst thou gain the Enlightenment of My Splendour?

51. O Son of Man!

My Calamity is My Providence. Without, it is fire and vengeance; within, it is Light and Mercy. Therefore welcome it with joy, that thou mayest become Everlasting Light and an Eternal Spirit. This is my Command; know thou it.

52. O Son of Humanity!

If good fortune come to thee, let it not rejoice thee; if humiliation overtake thee, mourn not because of it; for verily there shall be a time when both shall cease and be no more.

53. O Son of Existence!

If thou art stricken with poverty, sorrow not; for verily riches shall one day be thine. Fear not abasement, for exaltation shall be thy portion.

54. O Son of Existence!

If thou lovest the Ancient and Unending Kingdom, the Unpassing and Eternal Life, turn from this transient and mortal state.

55. O Son of Existence!

Let this world not engross thee. Verily fire is the test of gold; with gold We prove the hearts of men.

56. O Son of Man!

Thou desirest gold, but I desire thy separation from it. Thou hast thought to find thy riches in heaping it together; I know that to purify thyself from it is thy wealth. By My Life! That is thine imagining, this My knowledge; how can thy thought agree with Mine?

57. O Son of Man!

Distribute the gold which I have given thee among My Poor, that thou mayest in Heaven give from the Treasures of Exaltation which have no end, from the Stores of Glory which cannot be exhausted. But by My Life! The sacrifice of thyself is more glorious, couldst thou behold it with Mine Eye.

58. O Son of Humanity!

The temple of thy life is My Throne. Cleanse it utterly, that I may occupy it.

59. O Son of Existence!

Thy heart is My House; sanctify it, that I may enter it. Thy spirit is an aspect of My Essence; purify it for Mine Appearance.

60. O Son of Man!

Put thy hand into My Treasury, that I may raise My Head, shining with brilliancy, from above thy treasures.

61. O Son of Man!

Ascend to My Heaven that thou mayest come near to Me, that thou mayest drink from the Pure Wine which has no likeness—from the Everlasting Cup of Glory.

62. O Son of Man!

Many are the days that thou occupiest thyself with the superstitions and imaginings of thy fancy. How long wilt thou thus sleep upon thy bed? Lift thy head; for verily the Sun has arisen and ascended to the zenith, that He may shine upon thee with the Light of His Splendour.

63. O Son of Man!

Enlightenment has come to thee from the Horizon of the Mount, the Spirit of Holiness has breathed from the Sinai of thy heart. Therefore cleanse thyself from hindrances and imaginings; enter into the Court that thou mayest be prepared to meet Me—that thou mayest be fitted for the Everlasting Life where no trouble, weariness or death can befall thee.

64. O Son of Man!

My Eternity is My Creation and I have created it for thee; therefore make it the garment of thy temple. My Oneness is Mine Invention and I have invented it for thee; therefore clothe thyself with it. Thus mayest thou be the Arising-place of My Omnipresence forever.

65. O Son of Man!

My Greatness is My Gifts to thee, My Majesty is My Mercy to thee; but that which is due to Me none can realise or comprehend. I have kept it in the treasures of My Secrets, in the stores of My Mysteries—as a kindness to My Worshipers and a Mercy to My Creatures.

66. O Children of the Unseen Essence!

Ye will be hindered from loving Me—your hearts will be disturbed when I am mentioned, for the mind cannot grasp Me, the heart cannot encompass Me.

67. O Son of Splendour!

By My Spirit and by My Providence! By My Mercy and by My Splendour! All that which I have made known unto thee by the Tongue of Might and written for thee with the Pen of Power, is revealed according to thy place and station, not according to My Supreme Reality.

68. O Children of Men!

Know ye why I created ye from one dust? That no one should glorify himself over the other, that ye should always bear in mind the manner of your creation. Since I have created ye from one substance, it behooves ye to be as one, walking with common feet, eating with one mouth, living in one land; until in your natures and your deeds the signs of the Unity and the essence of the Oneness shall appear. This is My advice to ye, O ye People of Light! Profit by it, that ye may pluck the fruits of Holiness from the Trees of Might and Power.

69. O Children of the Spirit!

Ye are my Treasuries; for in ye have I stored the Pearls of my Secrets, the Gems of My Knowledge. Guard them, lest the unbelievers among My People, the wicked ones among My Creatures, should discover them.

70. O Son of Him Who stands in His own Essence in the Kingdom of Himself!

Know that I have bestowed the Fragrance of Holiness upon thee, have accomplished the Utterance unto thee, have perfected all Grace for thee, have willed for thee what I have willed for Myself. Therefore dwell in Me with love and gratitude.

71. O Son of Man!

On the tablet of thy soul write all that I have enjoined upon thee, with the ink of Light; and if thou canst not, write it with ink taken from the essence of thy heart; and if still thou canst not, write it with the red ink shed in My Cause, which verily is dearer to Me than all else; that its radiance may be confirmed for ever.

Abdu'l-Baha

Selections from the Writings of Abdu'l-Baha

I

I am ever anticipating joyous news from America, hoping that all the newspapers and journals might write of the Bahais in the following terms: "These people are distinguished in all qualities; they have pure intentions; they are truthful to all humanity; they are trustworthy; they exercise kindness toward all mankind; and with heart and soul and life they are engaged in service; they depend upon God; they are severed from the attachments of this world; albeit they are all engaged in some profession or work; they serve real civilization; in reality they are civilized people; they fear nothing whatever; night and day their thoughtful attention is devoted to philanthropic deeds; they wish no harm to anyone; they do not annoy anybody; they put forth efforts in general philanthropy; their greatest and highest desire is that bias may be removed from among the nations and sects of the world; that all mankind may be united with each other; that all wars and battles may be abolished from among the nations and powers of the world; that the standard of universal peace or the Most Great Peace shall be raised; that estrangement may cease entirely; that no religious fanaticism, racial or patriotic bias shall exist, for all are the creatures of God, and all are the signs of the Power of God.

II

In short, we hope that the beloved of God may raise the

standard of the solidarity of mankind in the center of the world; that all nations will unite and agree, gather together under the Blessed Banner attaining to the happiness of the world and the Kingdom.

III

Through the Protection and Help of the Blessed Perfection, you must conduct and deport yourselves in such a manner that you may stand out among other souls distinguished by a brilliancy like unto the Sun. If anyone of you enters a city he must become the center of attraction because of the Sincerity, Faithfulness, Love, Honesty, Fidelity, Truthfulness and Loving Kindness of his disposition and nature toward all the inhabitants of the world. That the people of the city may all cry out: "This person is unquestionably a Bahai. For his manners, his behavior, his conduct, his morals, his nature and his disposition are of the attributes of the Bahais." Until you do attain to this Station, you have not fulfilled the Covenant and the Testament of God.

IV

The Blessed Perfection has freed the necks from the bonds and fetters and released all from racial attachments by proclaiming—"Ye are all the fruits of one tree, and the leaves of one branch." Be ye kind to the human world, and be ye compassionate to the race of man. Deal with the strangers as you deal with the friends. Be ye gentle toward the outsiders as you are toward the beloved ones. Know the enemy as the friend, look upon the Satan as upon the Angel, receive the unjust with the utmost love like unto a faithful one, and diffuse far and wide the fragrances of the Musk of the gazelles of Kheta and Khotan to the nostrils of the ravenous wolves. Become ye a shelter and asylum to the fearful ones. Be ye a cause of tranquility and ease to the souls and hearts of the agitated ones. Impart ye strength to the helpless ones. Become ye a treasury of wealth to the indigent ones. Be ye a remedy and antidote to the afflicted ones; and a physician and nurse to the sick ones. Serve ye for the promotion of Peace and Concord, and establish in this transitory world the foundation of Friendship, Fidelity, Reconciliation and Truthfulness.

V

O ye friends of God! Be kind to all peoples and nations; have love for all of them; exert yourselves to purify the hearts as much as you can; and bestow abundant effort in rejoicing the souls. Be ye a sprinkling of rain to every meadow and the water of life to every tree. Be ye as fragrant musk to every nostril and a soul-refreshing breeze to every invalid. Be ye a spring to every thirsty one, a wise guide to every one led astray, an affectionate father or mother to every orphan, and in the utmost joy and fragrance, as son or daughter to every one bent with age. Be ye a rich treasure to every indigent one; consider love and union as a delectable paradise, and count annoyance and hostility as the torment of hell-fire. Exert with your soul; seek no rest in body; supplicate and beseech with your heart and search for Divine Assistance and Favor; in order that ye may make this world the Paradise of Abha and this terrestrial globe the Arena of the Supreme Kingdom. If ye make an effort, it is certain that these lights shall shine, and this cloud of mercy shall rain, this soul-nourishing breeze shall waft, and the scent of this most fragrant musk be diffused.

Shine ye like unto the Sun and roar and move like unto the Sea; impart life to mountain and desert like unto clouds; and, similar to the vernal breeze, bestow freshness, grace and elegance to the trees of human temples.

VI

Praise be to God that the divine cause in this Bahai dispensation is one of absolute love and of pure spirituality. It is not of this kingdom the earth, for it is not war and distress, nor the oppression of one people by another. Its army is the love of God, its victory is the ecstacy of the knowledge of God; its battle is that of Truth, the exposition of the Word; its warfare is against selfishness; its patience is its reserve; its entire meekness is its conquering power, and its love for all is a glory forevermore. In a word it is a spirit and it is love.

It is for us to consider how we may educate men that the darkness of ignorance and heedlessness may disappear and that the radiance of the kingdom may encompass the world; that the nations of men may be delivered from selfish ambition and strife, and be revivified by the fragrance of God; that animosity and hatred may be dispersed and wholly disappear, while the attracting power of the love of God so completely unites the hearts of men, that all hearts beat as a single heart; that the arteries of all mankind may pulsate with the love of God; that contention and war may utterly pass away, while peace and reconciliation lift their standard in the midst of the earth and men become enamoured of one another; that the joys of spirituality may prevail over material pleasure; that East and West may delight in one another as lovers, and North and South embrace each other in closest affection; that the visible world be the mirror of the world of the Kingdom; that the image of the Supreme Concourse may be reflected in all gatherings of men; that the earth may be changed into the paradise of the Glorious One, and the Divine Jerusalem embrace the terrestrial globe.

VII

Beware! Beware! of differences! By differences the Temple of God is razed to its very foundation; and by the blowing of the winds of disagreement the Blessed Tree is prevented from producing any fruit. By the intense cold of the diversity of opinions the rose garden of Unity is withered and the fire of the Love of God is extinguished.

VIII

The quintessence of Truth is this: We must all become united and harmonized in order to illumine this gloomy world; to abolish the foundations of hostility and animosity from among mankind; to perfume the inhabitants of the universe with the Holy Fragrance of the nature and disposition of the Beauty of Abha; to enlighten the people of the East and West with the light of Guidance; to hoist the tent of the Love of God and suffer each and all to enter under its Protection; to bestow comfort and tranquillity to everyone under the shade of the Divine Tree; to astonish the enemy by the manifestation of the utmost love; to make the ravenous and blood-thirsty wolves to be the gazelles of the meadow of the Love of God; to administer the taste of nonresistance to the tyrant; to teach the long-suffering and resignation of the martyrs to the murderer; to spread the traces of Oneness, to chant the praises and glorifications of the Glorious Lord; to raise the voice of Ya Baha'u'l-Abha to the Supreme Apex and to reach the ears of the inhabitants of the Kingdom with the outcry "Verily the earth is illumined by the Lights of its Lord." This is Reality! This is Guidance! This is Service! This is the consummation of the perfection of the realm of humanity.

IX

Baha'u'llah made the utmost efforts to educate his people and incite them to morality, the acquisition of the sciences and arts of all countries, kindly dealing with all the nations of the earth, desire for the welfare of all peoples, sociability, concord, obedience, courtesy, instruction of their children, production of what is needful for the human race, and inauguration of true happiness for mankind.

X

We were made to be happy and not sad; for joy, not for sorrow. Happiness is life; sadness is death; spiritual happiness is eternal life. It is a light that the night does not extinguish; it is an honor that shame does not follow, an existence which is not resolved into annihilation! For happiness, the worlds and contingent beings have been created.

XI

The hearts should be purified and cleansed from every trace of hatred and rancor and enabled to engage in truthfulness, conciliation, uprightness and love toward the world of humanity; so that the East and the West may embrace each other like unto two lovers, enmity and animosity may vanish from the human world, and the Universal Peace be established.

XII

The glory, happiness, honor and peace of man do not consist in personal wealth, but on the contrary, in sublimity of soul, nobility of resolution, extension of education and in the solution of the problem of life.

XIII

A man should be a constant source of well-being and contentment, and a ready help to prosperity for multitudes of people.

XIV

The sacred qualities of the people of Faith are justice, judgment, long-suffering, patience, kindness, faithfulness, sincerity, fidelity, love, benevolence, zeal, the protection of others, and humanity.

XV

Knowledge and wisdom, purity and faithfulness and

freedom of the soul, have not been and are not judged by outward appearance and dress.

XVI

Carnal desire is like a fire which has consumed a hundred thousand edifices built up by thoughtful sages; and even the sea of their sciences and arts has not been able to put out this blazing conflagration.

XVII

There is this condition that the central aims of morals should be wisdom and knowledge, and its controlling idea should be true moderation.

XVIII

Discover for yourselves the reality of things, and strive to assimilate the methods by which the means of life, of well-being, of noble mindedness and glory are attained among the nations and people of the world.

XIX

The other characteristics of progress are, the fear of God, the love of God in the love of mankind in general, long suffering, steadfastness, truth, compassion, generosity, bravery, boldness, perseverance, activity, purity, cheerfulness, modesty, zeal, resolution, high-mindedness, the cherishing of righteousness and wisdom, intellect, sobriety, true piety, and, above all, the fear of God within the heart.

XX

There is urgent need of widespread thought and study; and much wisdom and discrimination are required. Alas! my heart swells within me and is full of grief, because it cannot see that the people are devoting their care and energy to what today is worthy of both.

XXI

Even as avoiding and shunning the company of people and being harsh with them are the sure means of filling them with fear, so are love, kindliness, humility and gentleness the truest method of binding people's souls and attracting their hearts.

XXII

The first thing to be considered in every art before studying it is to what benefit comes from that art, and what fruit and result can be obtained. If a universal profit accrues to the majority of mankind from useful sciences surely a man should exert himself to study them with his whole soul. If the sole result of his study is to consist in useless reasonings, following after the imaginations of others, and becoming a center of quarrel and dispute out of which no one can derive any advantage—what is the sense of it, why should a man spend his life in empty discussion and argument?

71

XXIII

He who remaineth idle and indifferent, and continueth in his egoism, indulging constantly his carnal appetites, descendeth to the lowest abyss of degradation and ignorance. Lower is he than the most dangerous of savage beasts. For it is written: "These indeed are worse than brutes; and meaner than cattle in the sight of God."

XXIV

Exalt your ambition on high, and make your purposes excelling! How long will ye endure in sloth? How long in negligence? You can find nothing to be gained by idleness, except despair in this world and the next, and you can gain nothing except degradation and subjection by indulging in ignorance and superstition, and listening to the words of the thoughtless.

XXV

Therefore must we gird up the vesture of ambition round the loins of enthusiasm, and earnestly strive to seize the just causes of comfort, peace, happiness, knowledge, culture, art, honor, glory, for the benefit of all.

XXVI

All are servants of the One God—and God reigns over all and has pleasure in all alike. All men are of one family, the crown of humanity rests on the head of each man. In the eyes of the Creator all are equal. He is kind to all, He does not favor this nation or that nation, all are his creatures. If this is so, why should we divide one race from another, creating superstitions, differences between one people and another?

XXVII

Absolute equality amongst men; this would be impossible. There is needed some organization which will bring about an order in this disorder. Absolute equality is a mere dream, and impracticable. If absolute equality existed the whole order of the world would be destroyed. In mankind there is always a difference in degree. Since Creation men have never been the same. Some have superior intelligence, others are more ordinary and some are devoid of intellect. How can there ever exist equality between those who are clever and those who are not? Humanity is like an army. An army must have a general, captains and soldiers, each with their appointed duties, it cannot consist of generals only, or captains, or soldiers only; there must be degrees in the organization.

XXVIII

If women were educated with the same advantages as men, their capacity is the same and the result would be the same; in fact women have a superior disposition to men, they are more receptive, more sensitive, their intuition is more intense. The only reason of their present backwardness in some directions is because they have not had the same educational advantages as men.

If a mother is well educated, her children will also be

well taught. If the mother is wise, the children will be wise; if the mother is religious, the children will also be religious. If the mother is a good woman, then the children will also be good. The future generation depends then on the mothers of today. Is not this a vital position of responsibility for women?

Surely God does not wish such an important instrument as woman to be less perfect than she is able to become! Divine Justice demands that men and women should have equal rights, there is no difference between them, neither sex is superior to the other in the Sight of God.

XXIX

The world is like the body of man—it has become sick, feeble and infirm. Its eye devoid of sight, its ear become destitute of hearing and its faculties of sense are entirely dissolved. The friends of God must become wise physicians and care for and heal this sick person, in accord with the Divine Teachings, in order that it may perchance gain health, find eternal healing and that its lost powers may be restored; and that the person of the world may find such health, freshness and purity that it will appear in the utmost beauty and charm.

XXX

Wise men are as guiding lamps to the people. They are the stars of felicity in the horizon of tribes and nations; they are the Salsabil of life for the souls dead in ignorance and folly; and for those who wander and thirst in the wilderness of want they are a fresh spring of cooling water. They, indeed, have the truths of God's glorious Books, and are a living proof of the Unity of the Divine Spirit; to the diseased body of the world, they are skillful physicians, and are a true antidote to the poisoned soul of mankind. They are as an impregnable fortress protecting the world of humanity, and a sure refuge for those disturbed and disquieted by the forces of darkness and ignorance.

XXXI

Those great ministers who placed God's will before their own have been burning lamps of science among men of learning; they employ their wisdom for the general good of their countrymen. They prove themselves worthy examples of honest and virtuous endeavour, and with small hope of reward give their lives to the increase of public good. In their wisdom they deliver just ordinances to the people, setting the palm of peace among the nations; thus they attain the highest pinnacle of the mountain of glory and honor. Likewise the learned and famous Ministers, the repository of sound doctrine, and the wielders of the strong handle of piety and of the fear of God, place their trust in Him, and hold fast to the garment of salvation; and the mirror of their thoughts is adorned with the signs of sublime realities, and reflect the sun of universal knowledge. So they are diligently engaged, both night and day, in acquiring useful sciences and teaching and educating their chosen pupils.

XXXII

Friends of God, set forth the example of Justice! Justice is a Universal Quality. From the highest to the lowest, Justice should be sacred; from sovereign to the merchant, the Minister of State to the artisan, all must be just. Be just, respect the rights of each man, "do unto others what you would have them do unto you." A workman who commits an injustice is as much to blame as a tyrant. Each one of us can choose between justice and injustice.

I hope you will be just in your relations with others, that you will never harm your fellows, that you will respect the rights of all men, and above all, consider the rights of others before your own.

XXXIII

The Universal Principles which are the foundation of the Religion of God are laid down, but the making of specific laws which are subdivisions and ramifications is apportioned to the House of Justice. The wisdom of this is that this world never moves for a long period in one form. The House of Justice will make laws applicable to the exigencies and requirements of the time. Its members will not form institutions according to their own opinion and thought. The Most Great House of Justice enacts laws and statutes by the power of inspiration and confirmation of the Holy Spirit and is under the protection of God.

XXXIV

There are two great Banners which overshadow the crown of every sovereign; the first is that of Wisdom, the second that of Justice, which iron mountains cannot resist and which the "Wall of Alexander" will be powerless to stand against. With perfect ease will they penetrate into the states, the pillars of the world.

XXXV

How noble and excellent is man, if he only attains to that state for which he was designed. And how mean and contemptible, if he close his eyes to the public weal, and spend his precious capacities on personal and selfish ends. The greatest happiness lies in the happiness of others.

XXXVI

There can be no true satisfaction or contentment apart from the general prosperity.

XXXVII

We ask what deeds in the world could be greater than working in the public interests? Can any higher career be imagined than this, that a man should devote himself to the cause of the education, progress, glory and prosperity of the servants of God? No, in God's name! It is the greatest pious deeds that the blessed souls should take hold of them that are powerless by the hands, and deliver them from ignorance, degradation and poverty, and filled with sincere purpose for the sake of God, should gird up the loins of their ambition in the service of all people, forgetting their own worldly advantage and striving for the common good. As it is written: "And prefer others over thyself, even though there be poverty amongst them; the best of men are those who do good to their fellows, and the worst are those who do harm to them."

XXXVIII

Blessed is the man who forgets his own self-interest, like the Beloved Ones of the Threshold of God, and throws the ball of resolution onto the race ground of the common interest! Thus by tbe divine bounty and heavenly assistance, he will cause the glorious nation again to attain the Zenith of its former Grandeur, and these desolate regions to become refreshed by new life! So that, as the Nature-renewing Spring, he will give to the trees of Human souls the Holy blessings of spiritual leaves, flowers and fruits!

XXXIX

The differences in languages cause disunion between nations. There must be one universal auxiliary language. The diversity of Faiths is also a cause of separation. The true foundations of all faiths must be established, the outer differences abolished. There must be a Oneness of Faith. To end all these differences is a very hard task.

XL

It is God's will that the differences between nations should disappear. Those who help the cause of Unity, are doing God's work. Unity is the Divine Bounty of this brilliant century. Praise be to God there are many

Societies and many meetings held for Unity. Hatred is not so much the cause of separation now as it used to be; the cause of disunion now is mostly prejudice.

XLI

When one family is well united, great results are obtained. If this circle of unity be widened so as to include and control the interests of an entire village to the extent that all the members of its population are fully united and in perfect accord, the results will be proportionately greater; the fruits thereof will be accordingly.

Now widen the circle again! Let a city be united and the results will be still greater. Widen the circle yet more and have the people of a country united; then, indeed, important results shall be forthcoming. And if a Continent is fully united and will unite all the other Continents, then is the time when the greatest result shall be obtained.

Now consider, if Spiritual Unity be accomplished, what results will be forthcoming! If souls who are sons of the Kingdom be united, great shall be the results. Then the Divine Confirmations will become fully established, and their hearts and spirits will attain a remarkable illumination.

XLII

The existent world needs a uniting power to connect nations. There are various uniting powers in the world. One is patriotism, as in America, where people from different countries have united and made a nation. Another means of union is war, as when two nations unite to make war upon a third. A third uniting power is self-benefit, as is seen in trade and commerce. A fourth means of union is that furnished by ideals, different nations or different peoples having one aim or intention unite. All these uniting powers are ineffective and perishable; the only uniting power which can connect all hearts and last forever is faith in God and love for him. This is the only enduring power, the one that never perishes.

XLIII

It is plain and manifest that the surest means towards the well-being and prosperity of men, and towards the highest object of civilization, the liberty of the citizen, are love and friendship and the most intimate union between all individuals of the human race. Nothing in the world can be imagined or rendered easy without union and agreement; and the true divine religion is the most perfect cause of friendship and union in the world.

XLIV

Today in the world of existence there is no more important and greater cause than this Peace Movement, for it is conducive to the promotion of happiness in the commonwealth of humanity and is the cause of tranquility of all the nations and countries and the prosperity of the individuals of the human world. What cause is greater than this? It is evident that it has the utmost importance, nay, rather, it will be the cause of the illumination of the East and the West and the reason for the manifestation of the Countenance and the

Face of God in the world of humanity and the appearance of infinite affections.

XLV

The matter of international peace was instituted by His Highness, Baha'u'llah, sixty years ago in Persia in the year 1851, A. D. From that time innumerable epistles and tablets were spread first in Persia and then in other parts of the world, until about fifty years ago He clearly stated this matter of universal peace in the Book of Aqdas and has commanded all the Bahais to serve faithfully with heart and soul in this great cause, give up their possessions and wealth for it and sacrifice their lives in case of necessity. He has taught them to spread the unity of nations and religions and proclaim in all the regions of the world the oneness of the kingdom of humanity.

XLVI

About fifty years ago in the Book of Aqdas, Baha'u'llah commanded the people to establish the Universal Peace and summoned all the nations to the Divine Banquet of International Arbitration so that the questions of boundaries, of national honor and property and of vital interests between nations might be decided by an arbitral court of justice; and that no nation dare to refuse to abide their decisions. If any quarrel arise between two nations it must be adjudicated by this international court and be arbitrated and decided upon like the judgement rendered by the judge between two individuals. If at any time any nation dares to break such a treaty all the other nations must arise to put down this rebellion.

XLVII

How many thousands of men there are, who, instead of devoting themselves to the useful arts of peace, are daily employing their keenness and industry to the invention of new deadly instruments of war, which are to be the means of shedding the blood of their fellow-creatures with greater facility and profusion! Every day some such new and deadly weapon is being invented and, as the old ones cannot compete with the new, the European governments are constantly being obliged to abandon the older fashioned armaments and to make ready new ones.

XLVIII

Yea, the true civilization will raise its banner in the center of the world, when some noble kings of high ambitions, the bright Suns of the world of humanitarian enthusiasm, shall, for the good and happiness of all the human race, step forth with firm resolution and keen strength of mind and hold a conference on the question of universal peace; when keeping fast hold of the means of enforcing their views they shall establish a union of the states of the world, and conclude a definite treaty and strict alliance between them upon conditions not to be evaded. When the whole human race had been consulted through their representatives and invited to corroborate this treaty, which verily would be accounted sacred by all the peoples of the earth, it would be the duty of the united powers of the world to see that this great treaty should be strengthened and should endure.

XLIX

In such a universal treaty the limits of the borders and boundaries of every state should be fixed, and the customs and laws of every government; all the agreements and the affairs of state and the arrangements between the various governments should be propounded and settled in due form; the size of the armaments for each government should likewise be definitely agreed upon, because if in the case of any state there were to be an increase in the preparation for war, it would be a cause of alarm to other states. At any rate the basis of this powerful alliance should be so fixed that, if one of the states afterwards broke any of the articles of it, the rest of the nations of the world would rise up and destroy it. Yea, the whole human race would band its forces together to exterminate it.

L

If so great a remedy should be applied to the sick body of the world, it would certainly be the means of continually and permanently healing its illness by the inculcation of universal moderation. Reflect that, under such conditions of life, no government or kingdom would need to prepare and accumulate war materials, or would need to pay heed to the invention of new weapons of offense for the vexation and hurt of mankind. On the contrary, they would only require a few soldiers, as a means of assuring the safety of the state and punishing the wicked and rebellious and preventing the growth of sedition. Not more than these few would be needed.

LI

In the first place, therefore, the servants of God—that is to say, all the inhabitants of a state—would be freed from bearing the burden of the tremendous expense of an army; in the second, the many persons who now devote their lives to the invention of fresh instruments of war would no longer waste their time upon such work, which but encourages ferocity and bloodthirstiness, and is repugnant to the universal ideal of humanity—on the contrary, they would then employ their natural gifts in the cause of the general well-being and would contribute towards the peace and salvation mankind. All the rulers of the world will then be settled on peaceful thrones amid the glory of a perfect civilization, and all the nations and peoples will rest in the cradle of peace and comfort.

LII

Some persons who are ignorant of the world of true humanity and its high ambitions for the general good, reckon such a glorious condition of life to be very difficult, nay rather impossible to compass. But it is not so. Far from it. For by the grace of God, and by the testimony of the Beloved, those near the threshold of the Creator, and by the incomparably high ambitions of the souls that are perfect, and the thoughts and opinions of the wisest men of age, there never has been and is not now anything improbable and impossible in existence. What are required are the most resolved determination and the most ardent enthusiasm. How many things which in ancient times were regarded as impossibilities, of such a kind that the intellect could hardly conceive them, we now perceive to have become quite simple and easy! Why then should this great and important matter of universal peace, which is verily the sun amongst the lights of civilization, the cause of honor, freedom and salvation for all, be considered as something improbable of realization?

LIII

It is evident that the honor and greatness of man have not arisen through bloodthirstiness, the destruction of cities and kingdoms, the ruining and murdering of armies aud peoples. On the contrary the cause of high-mindedness and prosperity is based upon the cherishing of justice and the sympathy of one's fellow-citizens, from the highest to the lowest, upon building up the kingdom, cities and villages, the suburbs and the country, and upon the freedom and quiet of the servants of God in laying down the foundations of the principles of progress and in the extension of the common weal, the increase of wealth and general prosperity.

LIV

Yea, the expansion of the world and the subduing thereof is praised; yea, even war is sometimes the great foundation of peace, and destroying is the cause of rebuilding. If, for example, a great sovereign should wage war against a threatening foe, or for the unification of the whole body of people and divided kingdom he may urge the steed of resolution into the race course of bravery and courage; in short, this war may be essentially attuned to the melodies of peace; and then verily this fury is kindness itself and this opposition is the essence of justice itself and this war is the source of reconciliation. Today, the true duty of a powerful king is to establish a universal peace; for verily it signifies the freedom of all the people of the world.

LV

Some are too rich, some are too poor, some have millions and some have nothing. An organization is necessary to control this state of affairs. It is necessary to limit riches and it is necessary to limit poverty. Either extreme is wrong. There should be a medium state. If it is right for a capitalist to possess a great fortune, then it is also just that a laborer should have means of existence. If poverty is allowed to reach a condition of starvation it proves that there is a tyranny. Men must see that this does not happen in any case. There must be special laws. The rich must give of their plenty. If they have more than they need they must think of those who are in want.

LVI

The government of a country should make laws which conform to the Divine Law. The Law of God exacts that there should be neither excessive wealth nor excessive poverty.

LVII

Interference with the religion and faith in every country causes manifest detriment, while justice and equal dealing towards all peoples on the face of the earth are the means whereby progress is effected.

LVIII

The conscience of man is sacred and to be respected; and liberty thereof produces widening of ideas, amendments of morals, improvement of conduct, disclosure of the secrets of creation, and manifestation of the hidden verities of the contingent world.

LVIX

Religion is the basis of the happiness of the world of humanity. Merciful attributes are the best adornments for man. Science holds the next position to Religion. Science is conducive to the happiness of the world of humanity next in degree to Religion. If a nation be well qualified with education and yet dispossessed of good morals, it will not attain happiness. If that same nation be dispossessed of education, but possessed of moral training, it will be capable of accomplishing philanthropic deeds. When Religion and Science go hand in hand, then will it be light upon light.

LX

Two Things are most necessary to the political realm:

I. The Legislative Power
II. The Executive

The center of the executive power is the government, and the legislative power lies in the hands of thoughtful and wise men. On the other hand, if these strong pillars and firm foundations are not complete and comprehensive, how can it be supposed that there will be safety and salvation for the nation? Thus it is of the utmost importance to establish an assembly of learned men, who, being proficient in the different sciences and capable of dealing with all the present and future requirements will settle the questions in accordance with forbearance and firmness.

LXI

The characteristic of progress and self-perfecting consists in the observance of justice and righteousness.

LXII

Another characteristic of progress consists in the earnest and sincere development of public education, in the teaching of all the useful sciences and in encouraging the people to adopt the modern inventions, in extending the spheres of the arts and commerce, and endeavoring to induce them to adopt the methods by which the country may be enriched.

LXIII

Yea, verily, wealth and riches are worthy of praise if they be justly partitioned amongst the nation, but if some few be possessed of great riches, and many be reduced to poverty, then is the rich man's gold deprived of all its worth. But if great wealth be employed in the propagation of science, in the establishment of schools and colleges, in the nurture of the arts, in the education of orphans and the care of the needy, in brief, for the public benefit, then shall its possessor be accounted great, both in the sight of God and man.

LXIV

Riches are earned by personal effort with Divine assistance, in various trades, agriculture and the arts, and, rightly administered, are justly deserving of praise, forasmuch as if a wise and discerning man acquire them, they become a ready means of benefit to the state.

LXV

It is most clear and manifest that national affairs will never revolve around their proper axis until the whole people have received instruction, and public thought has been directed to a single end.

LXVI

The most important of all the matters in question, and that with which it is most specially necessary to deal effectively, is the promotion of education.

LXVII

No freedom or salvation could be imagined in the case of any nation which had not progressed in this greatest and most important point; just as the greatest cause of degradation and decadency of every nation is bigotry and ignorance.

LXVIII

If necessary, make this even compulsory, for not until the veins and tendons of the nation stir with life, will any study and adoption of improvements be of any avail, because the nation is unto the body, zeal and resolution are like unto the soul, so that the soulless body cannot move.

LXIX

Certainly, it were possible to gather together the vigorous intellects and the far-seeing talents of the most eminent men in the country, as well as the perseverance and enthusiasm of the most prominent statesmen and the persuasive strength of the most intelligent and competent persons, who have knowledge of the great laws governing political affairs; and if with united endeavor and steadfastness they were to consider and discuss both the highest general principles and the smallest details; then perhaps, as the result of fruitful and righteous deliberation, there might be a general improvement in some of the national concerns. But the counsellors would, in most instances, be obliged to learn from other countries, because, during several centuries, millions of people lived and died, before the elements of modern progress came into existence.

LXX

It is as clear as noonday that it is lawful to acquire knowledge and the art of right government from foreign nations, so the public attention may be directed to these important questions and that these methods of reform may be made publicly known, and that, in a short period, by God's help, the prudent nation may become chief amongst peoples.

LXXI

No one must wonder at these statements, for the chief, nay, the universal purpose of establishing by great laws the principles and foundations of all kinds of civilization, is the happiness of human beings; and human happiness lies in being near to the "Threshold of the Almighty God," and in the well-being of all persons, whether of high or low station. And the perfecting of the morals of humanity is the chief means towards those ends. The outward trappings of civilization, without inward moral advancement, may be likened unto confused dreams which cannot be interpreted; and sensual enjoyment, apart from spiritual perfection, is like unto the mirage which he that is athirst believes to be water. For, the fulfilling of the will and pleasure of God, and the advancement of the peace and well-being of the people cannot be perfectly achieved by external civilization alone.

LXXII

A man begins with a little selfish view of Good limited to himself; after a time, he learns more wisdom and his view of Good enlarges to his own household. Then, with more wisdom comes the realization that Good must include his family, no matter how large. Again more wisdom, and his family becomes his village, his village his city, and in turn, his city his country. But this is not enough; as his wisdom grows, his country becomes his continent, and his continent, the world; his family has become mankind. It is the duty of the Press to teach this wisdom to mankind, for it is the wisdom of God. It is the work of a true Press to teach this wisdom of God.

LXXIII

Those newspapers which strive to speak only that which is truth, which hold the mirror up to truth, are like the sun, they light the world everywhere with truth and their work is imperishable. Those who play for their own little selfish ends give no true light to the world and perish of their own futility. How were people to know the truth if it was veiled from them in their journals?

LXXIV

Firstly: The elected members must be God-fearing, high-minded and followers of the law.

Secondly: They should have an accurate knowledge of the Divine Commandments, of the most important fundamental matters and of the rules of the loosening and binding of domestic affairs and foreign relations; they should possess a knowledge of the science and arts, necessary to civilization, and finally be contented with the income derived from their personal property.

LXXV

But if, on the contrary, the members are mean, ignorant, having no knowledge of political economy, wanting in ambition, lacking in zeal, foolish, slothful, and seeking their personal or private advantages, then no good can possibly result from Assemblies so formed. Whereas, in former times, a poor man had to give a gratuity to one individual in order to obtain his rights, he might now be obliged to satisfy the demands of the entire body.

LXXVI

It is clearly shown that establishment of such assemblies will lead to justice and piety. Of this there can be no doubt. But what can bring the purposes of the Ministers and elected members to light? If they be men of sincere intention, good results and unexpected improvements should certainly follow, as a natural consequence; but if, on the other hand, they are unworthy of their trust, evil results must ensue.

LXXVII

It seems to me, right, that election of temporary members of the assemblies of the kingdom should depend upon the choice and satisfaction of the public, for members elected by the people are pledged to carry out their will, and to follow out their instructions.

LXXVIII

The ministers, and even the lowest officers of state, must be completely purified from all suspicion, and must assume the garment of chastity, and of pure life. And the improved condition we so earnestly desire will not have been attained until the regulation of public and private manners reach such a degree of perfection that it becomes impossible for any man to swerve one hair's breadth from the right path, even should he endeavor to do so; so that all government may be administered according to the laws of equity and justice, and that the responsible ministers find it impossible to swerve to the right or to the left, and of necessity pursue the way of righteousness.

LXXIX

The ways and means of producing happiness and good are capable of gross abuse; and depend upon the opinion, capability, piety, truthfulness, benevolence and the extent of zeal of the governed and their rulers.

LXXX

All partiality and perversion of justice by bribery, for personal liking or hatred, must be abolished, and both sides should be heard without favor; neither should the wicked be justified, nor the innocent condemned.

LXXXI

The hidden treasures of kings cannot be compared with

a drop of the water of science; not with the smallest cup of their learning; and the heaped-up talents of gold and silver cannot be equal to the solution of the least abstruse of their problems.

LXXXII

They will not seek wealth or self-advancement. Those kings and rulers whose fame for just government and greatness filled the world did not occupy themselves alone with their personal ambition and the acquirement of riches, but accounted the public weal and the increase of the inhabitants of their countries and the general treasury as their greatest care. Their glory was not bought with gold or silver, but was purchased by the soundness of their principles and the nobility of their aspirations. Such are those rulers who are benevolent and wise, whose dignity and real happiness lie in the well being of the public, whose ambition consists in diligently searching after such things as will justify them and their wealth and will bring happiness and peace upon the people.

LXXXIII

The learned men consider the pleasures of nations as the playthings of children, and account riches and worldly pomp the fit reward of the mean and ignorant. Like the birds, they are content with a few grains for their sustenance, but the melody of their wisdom and their knowledge will excite the astonishment of the intelligent and discerning among the sages of the world.

LXXXIV

The brightness of life hangs on Religion; and the progress, renown and happiness of people consist in keeping the commandments of God's Holy Books. To one who considers life as a whole, it is manifest that in this world, regarded both materially and spiritually, Religion embodies the chief, infrangible foundation of things, and the highest, most righteous and impregnable principles attainable in creation; it embodies the whole of the ideal and formal perfections, and it is the controller of the civilization and the prosperity of all mankind.

LXXXV

Is religion the real fundamental principle of humanity and civilization? or is it—as Voltaire and such as he have thought it to be—the destroyer of the essentials of the success, peace and well-being of mankind?

LXXXVI

At the bottom of religion is sincerity; to be more explicit, the religious man must be free from all personal hatred and should exert himself for the good of the community. Only by the agency of true religion is it possible for men to close their eyes to their own personal advantages and to sacrifice their own personal benefit for the general well-being. For self-love is inherent in the disposition of man, and it is impossible for him to neglect his own casual temporal advantages unless he has the hope of a great proportionate reward in the next world.

LXXXVII

In brief, every benefit to mankind is obtained by the graces of the Divine Religion, because it leads the truly religious souls to sincere purposes, high ambitions, spotless chastity and honor, kindliness and mercy, fidelity, to promise, freedom of rights and liberality; justice to all classes and conditions of men, manliness, generosity, courage, resolute endeavor and striving for the good of all the servants of God. Furthermore, it induces the various pleasing customs of humanity which are the bright candle of civilization.

LXXXVIII

Can it be said that the principles of the Divine Religion are opposed to the giving of encouragement and stimulation for the study of useful sciences and the spreading of general education, a knowledge of the practical advantages of natural philosophy, the extension of the domain of handicrafts and the increase of the materials of commerce and national wealth? Or are the disposition of the military forces in the cities, the planning of suburbs and villages, the repairing of roads and bridges and the construction of railways in order to facilitate the means of transport and the traveling of the inhabitants of a country—are these opposed and repugnant to the Threshold of Unity? Or are the discovering of abandoned mines which are a great source of wealth to a state and nation, and the founding of works and factories, which are a means of well-being, peace, and riches for a whole nation, the encouragement of the originating of new handicrafts, and the advancement of the progress of home trade—are these adverse to the commandments of the Lord of Creation?

LXXXIX

The accessories of the Mashriqu'l-Adhkar are numerous. Among them are the School for Orphans, the great College for the Higher Arts, Hospital, Home for the Cripples, and Hospice. The doors of these places are to be opened to all nations and religions.

XC

Although the Temple is the place of worship, with it is connected the Hospital, Pharmacy, Hospice, School for Orphans and University for the Study of Higher Sciences.

XCI

It requires a very large piece of ground so that Hospitals, Colleges, Hospice, School for Orphans and the Mashriqu'l-Adhkar for worship can be built. These buildings must be on one piece of ground but separated from each other by meadows and gardens.

XCII

The Mashriqu'l-Adhkar must have nine sides, doors, fountains, paths, gateways, columns and gardens, with the ground floor, galleries and dome and in design and construction must be most beautiful and artistic.

XCIII

The most important point is that from the Mashriqu'l-Adhkar must go forth not only spiritual necessities, but also the material needs, such as hospitals, schools, orphanages, hospices, etc.

XCIV

The Mashriqu'l-Adhkar has important accessories which are accounted as the basic foundations. These are: School for Orphans, Hospital and Dispensary for the Poor, Home for the Crippled, College for the higher scientific education. In every place—
First, a Mashriqu'l-Adhkar must be formed.
Then a School for the Education of Orphans and Poor.
Then a Hospital and Dispensary must be established.
Then a Home for the Crippled.
Then a College for Higher Scientific Education.

XCV

The arrangement of the Mashriqu'l-Adhkar is such that it will exert the greatest influence upon the civilized world on account of many accessories. Among them are the following: School for Orphans, College for Higher scientific Education, Hospital, Home for the Cripples, and Hospice. When the Mashriqu'l-Adhkar, with its accessories, is founded in the world, aside from the religious and spiritual influence, it will have a tremendous effect upon civilization.

Spirit of the Age

Abdu'l-Baha

O Lord, Thou hast said in Thy manifest Book: *"God does not change that which a people have, until they change that which is within themselves. When men forgot God, He made them to forget their own reality."*
All the Teachings which have been given during past days are to be found in the Revelation of Baha'u'llah, but in addition to these this Revelation has certain new Teachings which are not to be found in any of the religious books of the past.

The oneness of the world of humanity is a Teaching of Baha'u'llah, for Baha'u'llah addresses Himself to mankind, saying: "Ye are all the leaves of one tree and the drops of one ocean." That is, the world of human existence is no other than one tree, and the nations or peoples are like unto different branches thereof. Thus Baha'u'llah presented the fact of the oneness of the world of humanity, while in all the past religious books humanity has been divided into two parts, one part looked upon as belonging to the faithful, the other part as belonging to the irreligious and infidel; the first part consigned to the Mercy of their Creator, the second part considered as objects of the Creator's Wrath. But His Holiness Baha'u'llah proclaimed the Oneness of the world of humanity, and this Teaching is unique to the Teachings of Baha'u'llah, for He submerged all mankind in the sea of Divine Generosity. At most, some of the people are asleep—they need to be awakened. Some are ill—they need to be healed. Some are children—they need to be trained.

A second Teaching newly revealed by Baha'u'llah is this: the injunction to investigate the Truth—that is, men are commanded not to follow blindly the ways of their ancestors. Nay, each must see with his own eyes, hear with his own ears, investigate the Truth for himself that he may attain the Truth by himself.

A third Teaching of Baha'u'llah which is new for this Day: that the foundation of all the religions of God is one and the same foundation, and that Oneness is the Truth, and the Truth is One, and cannot be made subject to division and plurality.

The fourth Teaching of Baha'u'llah special to this Day is that Religion must be the cause of unity, harmony and accord among men. If religion be the cause of inharmony, or leads men to separate themselves each from the other, creating conflict between them—then Baha'u'llah declares that irreligion is better than Religion.

A fifth Teaching of Baha'u'llah is new in this Day: that Religion must be in accord with science and reason. If a religion is not in conformity with science and reason—then it is superstition.

The sixth new Teaching of Baha'u'llah is the equality between men and women. All past Religions have established men above women.

The seventh new Teaching of Baha'u'llah is that prejudice and fanaticism—be it religious, sectarian, sectional, denominational or patriotic—is destructive of the foundation of human solidarity; wherefore men should release themselves from such bonds in order that the oneness of the world of humanity may become manifest.

The eighth of His Teachings is Universal Peace: that all men and nations should make peace; that there shall

101

be a Universal Peace amongst governments, Universal Peace amongst Religions, Universal Peace amongst races.

The ninth of these special Teachings is that all mankind—men and women everywhere—should acquire secular and spiritual knowledge, and that this education is one of the necessities of Religion.

The tenth Teaching concerns the solution of the economic question; for no religious books of the past Prophets speak of the economic question, while this problem has been thoroughly solved in the Teachings of Baha'u'llah.

The eleventh is the organization called the House of Justice, which is endowed with a political as well as spiritual function, and embodies both functions, and is protected by the preserving Power of Baha'u'llah Himself. A Universal or World House of Justice shall be established. That which it orders shall be the truth in explaining the commands of Baha'u'llah, and that which the House of Justice ordains concerning the commands of Baha'u'llah shall be observed by all.

But as to the most characteristic and specific Teaching which belongs to the Revelation of Baha'u'llah, which is new and not given by any of the Prophets of the past: it is the Teaching regarding the Center of the Covenant. To guard against all manner of differences, Baha'u'llah entered into a Covenant with all the people of the world, indicating the Person of the Interpreter of His Teachings. Be ye cognizant of this!

The world had, through rotten, outdated and blind imitations of truth, become like unto a dark night. The foundations of the Teachings of God had been totally forgotten. People had adhered to the shell and neglected the kernel. The nations, like wornout garments, had fallen into pitiful decay.

In this intense darkness the light of the Teachings of Baha'u'llah appeared and adorned the body of the world with a new robe. This new robe is the Divine Principles. A new cycle dawned with Baha'u'llah; creation was renewed; the world of humanity received a new spirit; the season of autumn passed away and the life-giving springtime was come. Everything was renewed. Sciences were reborn, thoughts remodeled, manners and habits changed, industry revolutionized, inventions multiplied.

All these renovations originate in the renewal of the splendid graces of the Lord of the Kingdom through which the universe was inspired. Therefore the essential matter is to release people entirely from traditional thoughts, so that their minds may be entirely concentrated in the new teachings. The teachings of Baha'u'llah constitute the spirit of the age and the light of this century.

Ye should strive with heart and soul so that those who are negligent may become cognizant, those who are asleep may become awakened, those who are ignorant may obtain wisdom, those who are blind may obtain sight, those who are deaf may receive hearing, and those who are dead may be revived. Ye should exhibit such strength of steadfastness as to astonish the world. The heavenly confirmations are with you in service to the Cause of God.

The Teachings of Baha'u'llah, like unto Spirit, shall penetrate the dead body of the World, and like unto an artery shall beat through the heart of the five continents.

At the Friends' Meeting House

St. Martin's Lane, London
Sunday, January 12th, 1913

About one thousand years ago a Society was formed in Persia called the Society of the Friends, who gathered together for silent communion with the Almighty.

They divided Divine Philosophy into two parts: one part the knowledge of which can be acquired through lectures and study in schools, and the second part that sought by the Illuminati, or followers of the Inner Light. The schools of this Philosophy were held in silence. Meditating, and turning their faces to the Source of Light, the mysteries of the Kingdom were reflected from that central Light into their hearts. All the divine problems were solved by this power of illumination.

This Society of Friends increased greatly in Persia, and their meetings take place even at the present time. Many books and epistles were written by their leaders. When the Friends assemble in their Meeting House, they sit in silence and contemplate. Their leader proposes a certain problem, saying to the assembly "This is the problem on which to meditate." Then, freeing their minds from everything else, they sit quietly and reflect, and before long the answer is revealed to them. Many abstruse divine questions are solved by means of this illumination.

Some of the great questions unfolding from the rays of the Sun of Reality upon the mind of man are: the problem of the reality of the spirit of man; of the origin of the spirit; of its birth from this world into the world of God; the question of the inner life of the spirit and its fate after ascension from the body.

They also meditate upon the scientific questions of the day, and these are likewise solved.

These people, who are called "Followers of the Inner Light," attain to a superlative degree of power, and are entirely freed from blind dogmas and imitations. Men rely on the statements of these people: by themselves, within themselves, they solve all mysteries.

If they find a solution through the assistance of the Inner Light, they accept it, and afterwards declare it; otherwise they would consider it a matter of blind imitation. They go so far as to reflect, upon the essential nature of the Divinity, of the divine Revelation, of the Manifestation of the Deity in this world. All the divine and scientific questions are solved by them through the power of the spirit.

Baha'u'llah says there is a sign from God in every phenomenon. The sign of the intellect is contemplation, and the sign of contemplation is silence, because it is impossible for a man to do two things at once—he cannot both speak and meditate.

It is an axiomatic fact that while you meditate you are speaking with your own spirit. In that state of mind you put certain questions to your spirit and the spirit answers: the light breaks forth and reality is revealed.

You cannot apply the name "man" to any being devoid of this faculty of meditation; without it man is a mere animal, lower than the beasts.

Through the faculty of meditation man attains to eternal life; through it he receives the breath of the Holy Spirit—the bestowals of the Spirit are given during reflection and meditation.

The spirit of man is itself informed and strengthened during meditation; through it affairs of which man knew nothing are unfolded before his view. Through it he receives divine inspiration, and through it he partakes of heavenly food.

Meditation is the key for opening the doors of mysteries. In that state man abstracts himself; in that state man withdraws himself from all outside objects; in that subjective condition he is immersed in the ocean of spiritual life and can unfold the secrets of things-in-themselves. To illustrate this, think of man as endowed with two kinds of sight: when the power of insight is being used the power of outward vision does not function.

This faculty of meditation frees man from the animal nature, discerns the reality of things, puts man in touch with God.

This faculty brings forth the sciences and arts from the invisible plane. Through the meditative faculty inventions are made possible, colossal undertakings are carried out. Through it governments can run smoothly. Through this faculty man enters into the very Kingdom of God.

Nevertheless some thoughts are useless to man: they are like waves moving in the sea without result. But if the faculty of meditation is bathed in the Inner Light and characterized with divine attributes, the results will be confirmed.

The meditative faculty is akin to the mirror; if you put it before earthly objects, it will reflect the earthly objects. Therefore if the spirit of man is contemplating earthly objects he will become informed of these.

But if you turn the mirror of your spirit heavenwards, the heavenly constellations and the rays of the Sun of Reality will be reflected in your hearts, and the virtues of the Kingdom will be obtained.

Therefore let us keep this faculty rightly directed—turning it to the divine Sun and not to earthly objects—so that we may comprehend the allegories of the Bibles, the mysteries of the Spirit, and discover the hidden secrets of the Kingdom.

May we indeed become mirrors reflecting the divine realities, and may we become so pure as to reflect the stars of heaven!

Bahai Prayers

Prayers of Baha'u'llah

I

I testify, O my God, that Thou hast created me to know Thee and to adore Thee. I testify at this instant to my powerlessness and to Thy Power; to my weakness and to Thy Might; to my poverty and to Thy Riches. There is no God but Thee, the Protector, the Self-Subsistent!

II

Glory be unto Thee, O God, for Thy Manifestation of Love to mankind. O Thou, Who art our Life and Light, guide Thy servants to Thy Way, and make them rich in Thee and free from all save Thee.

O God, teach them Thy Oneness, and give unto them a realisation of Thy Unity, that they may see no one save Thee. Thou art the Merciful and the Giver of Bounty.

O God, create in the hearts of Thy beloved the fire of Thy Love, that it may burn the thought of everything save Thee.

Reveal unto them, O God, Thy exalted Eternity, that Thou hast ever been and wilt ever be, and that there is no God save Thee. Verily in Thee will they find comfort and strength.

III

O my God, let my destiny, which is written by Thy Greatest Pen, be to obtain the blessings of the worlds to come and of the present one. I hereby bear witness that in Thy Hands are the reins of all things and that Thou changest them according to Thy Will, and that there is no God but Thee, for Thou art the One, the Almighty, the Faithful.

Thou art the One Who changest by His command the dishonoured to the highest state of honour, the weak to be strong, the failing to have power, the confused to be in peace and the doubting to have strong faith.

There is no God but Thee, Who art the Dearest and the Most Generous. The heavens of Thy Mercy and the oceans of Thy Bounty are so vast that Thou hast never disappointed those who begged of Thee, nor refused those who willed to come to Thee.

Thou art the Most Powerful, the Almighty!

IV

O my God! Make Thy Beauty to be my food, and let Thy Presence be my drink. Let my trust be in Thy Will, and my deeds according to Thy Command. Let my service be acceptable to Thee, and my action a praise to Thee. Let my help come only from Thee, and ordain my Home to be Thy Mansion, boundless and holy.

Thou art the Precious, the Ever-present, the Loving!

V

In Thy Name, the Sufficer, the Healer, the Fulfiller, the Loftiest, the Supreme, the Glory of the Glory!

I ask Thee by Thine Ancient Beauty, and I supplicate Thee by the Manifestation of Thy Greatest Majesty, and Thy Name, around which the Heavens of the Manifestations revolve, by which all sorrow will be turned into joy and all disease will be turned into health, and by which every sick, afflicted, unfortunate, and constrained one may be healed, to suffice to heal this weary sick-worn one of the seen and the unseen disease.

Verily Thou art the Powerful, the Conqueror, the Mighty, the Living, the Forgiver.

VI

Glory be to Thee, my God and my Beloved! Thy Fire is burning in me, O my Lord, and I feel its glowing in every member of my weak body. Every organ of my temple declares Thy Power and Thy Might, and every member testifies that Thou art powerful over all things. By Thy Strength I feel strong to withstand all trials and all temptations. Make firm Thy Love in my heart, and then I can bear all the swords of the earth. Verily every hair of my head testifies: "Were it not for trials in Thy Path I should not have appreciated Thy Love."

O my Lord, strengthen me to remain firm, to uphold the Hands of Thy Cause, and to serve Thee among Thy people. Thou art Loving! Thou art Bountiful!

Prayers of Abdu'l-Baha

I

O my God! O my God!

This, Thy servant, hath advanced toward Thee, is passionately wandering in the desert of Thy love, walking in the path of Thy service, anticipating Thy favors, hoping for Thy bounty, relying upon Thy Kingdom, and being exhilarated with the wine of Thy gift. O my God! Increase his fervor in Thy passion, his constancy in Thy praise and his ardor in Thy love. Verily, Thou art the Beneficent and endowed with great bounty! There is no God but Thee, the Forgiving, the Merciful!

II

O Lord, I have turned my face unto thy Kingdom of Oneness and am drowned in the sea of Thy mercy! O Lord, enlighten my sight by beholding Thy lights in this dark night, and make me happy by the wine of Thy love in this wonderful age! O Lord, make me hear Thy call, and open before my face the doors of Thy heaven, so that I may see the light of Thy glory and become attracted to Thy beauty!

Verily, thou art the Giver, the Generous, the Merciful, the Forgiving!

III

O my God! O my God! Glory be unto Thee for that Thou hast confirmed me to the confession of Thy Oneness, attracted me unto the word of Thy Singleness, enkindled me by the fire of Thy love, and occupied me with Thy mention and the service of Thy friends and maid-servants.

O Lord, help me to be meek and lowly and strengthen me in severing myself from all things and in holding to the hem of the garment of Thy Glory, so that my heart may be filled with Thy love and leave no space for the love of the world and the attachment to its qualities.

O God! Sanctify me from all else save Thee, purge me from the dross of sins and transgressions and cause me to possess a spiritual heart and conscience.

Verily Thou art merciful and verily Thou art the Generous, the Helper.

IV

I arise in Thy Shelter, and it behooveth him who seeketh Thy protection to be under the shield of Thy Guard, and in the Fortress of Thy Defence. O my Lord, enlighten me inwardly by the Lights of the Day-break of Thy Manifestation, as Thou hast enlightened me outwardly by the Light of the dawn of Thy Favour.

V

Praise be unto Thee, Oh my God, that Thou hast awakened me after my sleep, caused me to appear after my absence, and raised me from my insensibility. I arose facing the Lights of the Dawn of Thine Appearance, by which the horizons of the Heavens of Thy Power and Thy Majesty were enlightened, confessing Thy Signs, assured in Thy Book, and holding to Thy Rope.

I beg of Thee, by the Power of Thy Will, and by the Penetration of Thy Purpose, to ordain that which Thou hast showed me in my vision, as the most solid foundation for the dwelling place of Thy love in the hearts of Thy Friends, and the best cause for the appearance of Thy Favour and Thy Grace.

Oh my Lord, ordain to me, by Thy Supreme Pen, the blessings of the world to come, and the present one. I bear witness, that verily the reins of affairs are in Thy Grasp, and that Thou changest them as Thou desirest. There is no God but Thee, the Powerful and the Faithful.

Thou art the One whose Command changeth lowliness into might; weakness into strength; humility to authority; confusion to tranquility, and doubt to conviction. There is no God but Thee, The Glorious, The Generous. Disappoint not whosoever entreateth Thee, and forbid not whosoever desireth Thee. Ordain that which befitteth the Heaven of Thy Bounty, and the Ocean of Thy Generosity. Verily Thou art the Powerful, the Mighty.

VI

O Thou most kind Lord, this reverent assembly is calling on Thy name. These souls are seeking Thy good pleasure. They are seeking the prosperity of the world of humanity. O Lord, confer upon their souls life evermore. O Lord, forgive their sins and keep them in Thy protecting shade in both worlds. O Lord, confer upon them Thy great pleasure. All are servants of

117

international peace, all are servants of humanity. Thou art the Merciful, the Generous, the Forgiver, the Almighty, the Praiseworthy!.

VII

Thou are the Praiser and the Praised One. O my God, and my Master and my Desire. This, thy servant desireth to sleep in the shelter of Thy Mercy, and to rest under the shadow of the Dome of Thy Favour, assisted by Thy Protection and Thy Guard. O my Lord, I invoke Thee, by Thine Eye which sleepeth not, to protect mine eye from beholding aught beside Thee. Then increase its light by witnessing Thy Signs, and by looking towards the Horizon of Thy Manifestation. Thou art He before whose Appearances of Might, the existence of power is subdued.

There is no God but Thee, the Powerful, the Conqueror, the Chosen One.

VIII

O my God! my God! Thanks be to Thee for guiding me unto Thy Kingdom, for opening before my face the door of Thy guidance, enlightening my eyes with beholding Thy signs, and filling my heart with the feelings of Thy love.

O Lord! O Lord! Make me severed from the world and void of its conditions, attracted by the fragrances of Thy holiness among Thy maid-servants, free in heart, happy in soul, cheerful in mind, longing for the Kingdom of Thy Beauty, and glowing with the fire of Thy love in the world. Thus may I enkindle the light of guidance in the hearts of Thy servants.

Verily, Thou art the Powerful, the Bestower, the Precious, the Mighty!

IX

O Thou Heavenly Father!
Thou hast the hosts of the Kingdom and the spiritual angels. We, indigent souls are broken-winged birds; yet we yearn to soar toward the immensity of the Kingdom. We are thirsty fish; we seek the Sea of the Water of Life. We are the butterflies of the nether world; we long for the Lamp of the Realm on High. We are in the utmost weakness and feebleness; yet we are fighting against the armies of the world. Therefore, O Lord of Hosts! Confirm us so that the army of Light may become victorious and the legions of the darkness be defeated. Assist us in the service of the Kingdom and acquaint us with the Divine Mysteries. Rejoice us with the glad-tidings of the everlasting sovereignty and bestow upon us a portion and a share of the Life Eternal. Suffer the tongues to be unloosed and grant sight to the eyes; so that we may behold the world of the Kingdom and may praise with an eloquent speech Thy Beauty and Thy Perfection.
Verily, Thou art the Bestower and the Kind!

X

Cover the sins of the weak ones with the hem of the garment of Thy Mercy! Change the indifference of the heedless ones into the essence of fidelity, wisdom and understanding! Grant the souls a loftier effort and arouse a spiritual tumult in the minds so that they may sing the melody of the Supreme Realm, seek for a Glory

119

Everlasting, long for the delicacies of the New World, soar toward the Brightest Horizon, enter the congregation of the Almighty and become the recipients of the bestowals of the Kingdom! Thus will the dark world become luminous, the satanic field transformed into the courts of the Merciful, the mound of earth become the mound of Heaven and the terrestrial globe the Eternal Rose-garden. Verily, Thou art the Powerful, the Mighty, the Hearer, the Seer!

XI

O my God, my God!

I am a servant attracted to Thee, humbly coming to the door of Thy Oneness and addressing the kingdom of Thy mercy.

O my God, permit that I should be entirely Thine, occupied in thinking of Thee, inflamed by the fire of Thy love and separated from all except Thee, so that I may work in Thy Cause, spread Thy wisdom, transmit Thy knowledge and the joy of knowing Thee.

O my God, I am a flame lighted by the hand of Thy power. Do not permit that it be extinguished by the winds of trials. Increase my love for Thee, my ardor for the Beauty of Thy Oneness, the fire that burneth in me in the Sinai of Thy Singleness, and the eternal life in me, through Thy bounty and grace; for Thou art the Protector, the Watcher, the Pitiful and the Merciful!

XII

O my God, O my God! How can I choose to sleep whilst the eyes of the yearning ones are awaken because of separation from Thee, and how can I rest on the bed whilst the minds of Thy lovers are troubled by Thine Absence. O my Lord, I confide my spirit and my essence in the right hand of Thy Authority and Thy Security, and I lay my head on the bed by Thy Power; then raise it therefrom by Thy Will and Thy Desire. Verily Thou art the Protector, the Guardian, the Powerful and the Mighty.

By Thy Might, naught I desire from sleep, neither from waking, but that which Thou desirest. I am Thy servant, and in Thy Grasp. Confirm me to that whereby the scent of Thy Satisfaction is diffused. This is my hope, and the hope of those who are near to Thy Presence. Praise be unto Thee, O God of the creatures.

XIII

My Lord! My Lord! I praise Thee and I thank Thee for that whereby Thou hast favored Thine humble maid-servant, Thy slave beseeching and supplicating Thee, because Thou hast verily guided her unto Thine obvious Kingdom and caused her to hear Thine exalted Call in the contingent world and to behold Thy Signs which prove the appearance of Thy victorious reign over all things.

O my Lord, I dedicate that which is in my womb unto Thee. Then cause it to be a praiseworthy child in Thy Kingdom and a fortunate one by Thy favor and Thy generosity; to develop and to grow up under the charge of Thine education. Verily Thou art the Gracious! Verily Thou art the Lord of Great Favor!

XIV

O Thou Pure God! I am a little child; make Thou the

121

bosom of Thy Gift a dear resting-place of comfort, suffer me to grow and be nurtured with the honey and the milk of Thy love and train me under the breast of Thy knowledge; bestow Thou freedom while in a state of childhood and grant Thou excellence!

O Thou Incomparable One! Make me the confident of the Kingdom of the Unseen! Verily, Thou art the Mighty and the Powerful!

XV

O loving God! I am a young child, a suppliant, a captive. Be Thou my refuge, my support, my protector. I am in distress: give me the means of tranquillity. I am needy: bestow upon me the treasure of the Kingdom. I am dead: give me the Spirit of Life. I am weak: favor me with power and strength, so that I may be a maid-servant in Thy Threshold, with perfect purity and sanctity; sacrifice myself unto Thee, be quit of myself and seek Thee, walk in the path of Thy good pleasure, speak Thy secret and witness the signs of Thy Oneness wherever I look. O God! Make me ablaze, like unto the fire of Thy love, and make me free from attachment to this mortal world, until I find the peace of soul and the rest of conscience.

Thou art the Powerful, the Mighty! Thou art the Hearer, the Seer!

XVI

O God! Refresh and gladden my spirit. Purify my heart. Illumine my powers. I lay all my affairs in Thy hand. Thou art my Guide and my Refuge. I will not be sorrowful and grieved; I will be a happy and joyful being. O God! I will no longer be full of anxiety, nor will I let trouble harass me. I will not dwell on the unpleasant things of life.

O God! Thou art more friend to me than I am to myself. I dedicate myself to Thee, O Lord.

XVII

O Unequalled Lord!

For this helpless child be a Protector; for this weak and sinful one be kind and forgiving.

O Creator! Although we are but useless grass, still we are of Thy garden; though we are but young trees, bare of leaves and blossoms, still we are of Thy orchard; therefore, nourish this grass with the rain of Thy bounty; refresh and vivify these young, languishing trees with the breeze of Thy spiritual springtime.

Awaken us, enlighten us, sustain us, give us eternal life and accept us into Thy Kingdom!

XVIII

O God, O God! We are Thy humble and submissive servants, leaves of Thine exalted and verdant paradise, drops from the basins of Thine abundant mercy, and scattered particles flying about in Thy shining rays.

O Lord, O Lord, render us successful through Thy conquering power, in that which Thou lovest and approvest, so that we may become standards of guidance, signs of Thy Kingdom, the El-Abha, adore Thee, supplicate before the Kingdom of Thy mercy, beseech Thy realm of might, be submissive to Thy servants, humble before Thy maid-servants, severed from aught else save Thee, sincerely turned unto Thy face, aflame with the fire of Thy love, diffusing Thy

123

fragrances, united in Thy Cause, of one accord in Thy religion, and firm in Thy Covenant. O God, strengthen us through the fragrances of Thy sanctity, that we may become sanctified from the stain of egotism and lust, baptized with Thy Holy Spirit, with the fire of Thy love and the water of Thy bounty.

Verily, Thou art the Bestower, the Assister, the Confirmer, the Beneficent, the Merciful!

XIX

O my Lord! O my Lord!

Verily, I am one of Thy maid-servants, supplicating humbly before the Door of Thy Singleness, beseeching and humbling myself to Thee! O my Lord! Thanks be unto Thee for Thy greatest guidance and Thy greatest favor, which Thou hast assigned unto me and unto Thy worshiping maid-servants, whom Thou hast chosen to enter Thine exalted Kingdom and abide in Thy Paradise of El-Abha. O my Lord! Sanctify me from every worldly station in this primal life and purify me from all else save Thee, O Thou Great Giver! Exhilarate me with the wine of Thy love, O Thou Brilliant Countenance! Intoxicate me with the wine of sanctity, purity, unity and singleness, O Thou who attractest the hearts of the righteous by the magnet of favors, unto the Kingdom of El-Abha! O my Lord! Cause me to speak Thy praise, illumine my sight through the light of Thy knowledge, cause me to hear Thy Call, and quicken me with the spirit of Thy grace. Make me rejoiced at the melodies of the birds of Thy holiness, and make me a servant to Thy maid-servants. Cause my soul to be tranquilized, my heart attached, and my mind drawn to the light of thy guidance, which is shining unto all regions; so that I may walk in the path of Thy good pleasure, yield to Thy decree and be rejoiced at the most violent calamities, and that my breast may become dilated during every tribulation, even though the suffering is beyond endurance. Verily, thou art the Holy, the Pure, the Potent, the Powerful, the Exalted, the Great!

XX

O my God! O my God!
This, thy servant, is turning unto Thee, relying upon Thee and is believing in Thee and in Thy great signs. He hath indeed traversed lands and seas, desiring to reach Thy brilliant Holy Land and Thy perfuming dust, and hath advanced toward the lofty court of Thy mercy to worship Thine Exalted Word. O my God! Assist him, through the One Mighty in Power, to obey Thy command, to walk in the path of Thy good pleasure to supplicate before the Kingdom of Thy Oneness, to become severed from all else save Thee, to beseech Thy might, to be consumed by Thy love and to spread Thy commemoration, O Thou who grantest the wishes of every supplicant! Verily, Thou art the Powerful, the Mighty!

XXI

My Lord! My Lord!
Thou hast caused me to hear the Call, guided me unto the sea of favor, awakened me through Thy fragrant breeze, and quickened me by the spirit of Thy greatest guidance. I thank and praise Thee for this. O my Lord! O my Lord! Verily, I am athirst; do cause me to drink from the fountain of Thy grace. O my Lord! O my Lord! Verily, I am ill; do heal me by the antidote of Thy mercy.

O my Lord! O my Lord! Verily, I am sick; do cure me through Thy favor. O my Lord! O my Lord! I am needy; do enrich me through Thy compassion. And I am poor; render me prosperous by the treasury of Thy Kingdom. O my Lord! O my Lord! Increase my hope in the court of Thy holiness, and grant my wishes by thy favor and grace. Confirm me to deliver Thy Cause, enable me to call in Thy Name, and cause me to show forth the proofs of Thy Manifestation. Strengthen me to promote Thy Word, dilate my breast by serving Thy maid-servants and being humble and submissive before Thy beloved ones. O my Lord! Verily, I am impotent; do strengthen me by Thy power. I am lost in indigence; do confer on me Thy greatest favor. Make me as one of the maid-servants who diffuse Thy fragrances, who worship Thy Kingdom, who bow down in the worshiping-places of Thy unity, who kneel down on every dust which is related to the threshold of Thy beloved ones, and who serve in Thy vineyard, speak Thy praise and are attracted to Thy love. Verily, Thou are the Giver, the Powerful, the Mighty!

XXII

O my Lord! O my Lord!

This is a lamp lighted by the fire of Thy love and ablaze with the flame which is ignited in the tree of Thy mercy. O my Lord! Increase his enkindlement, heat and flame, with the fire which is kindled in the Sinai of Thy Manifestation. Verily, Thou art the Confirmer, the Assister, the Powerful, the Generous, the Loving!

XXIII

O my Lord, my Beloved, my Desire!

Befriend me in my loneliness and accompany me in my exile; remove my sorrow, cause me to be devoted to Thy Beauty, withdraw me from all else save Thee, attract me through Thy fragrances of holiness, cause me to be associated in Thy Kingdom with those who are severed from all else save Thee and who long to serve Thy Sacred Threshold and who stand to work in Thy Cause, and enable me to be one of Thy maid-servants who have attained to Thy good pleasure. Verily, Thou art the Gracious, the Generous!

XXIV

O my Lord!

Thou knowest that the people are encircled with pain and calamities and are environed with hardships and trouble. Every trial doth attack man and every dire adversity doth assail him like unto the assault of a serpent. There is no shelter and asylum for him except under the wing of Thy protection, preservation, guard and custody.

O Thou the Merciful One! O my Lord! Make Thy protection my armory, Thy preservation my shield, humbleness before the door of Thy Oneness my guard, and Thy custody and defense my fortress and abode. Preserve me from the suggestions of myself and desire, and guard me from every sickness, trial, difficulty and ordeal.

Verily, Thou art the Protector, the Guardian, the Preserver, the Sufferer, and verily, Thou art the Merciful of the Most Merciful!

XXV

O Compassionate God! Thanks be to Thee for Thou hast awakened and made me conscious. Thou hast given me a seeing eye and favored me with a hearing ear; hast led me to Thy Kingdom and guided me to Thy Path. Thou hast shown me the right way and caused me to enter the Ark of Deliverance. O God! Keep me steadfast and make me firm and stanch. Protect me from violent tests and preserve and shelter me in the strongly fortified fortress of Thy Covenant and Testament. Thou art the Powerful! Thou art the Seeing! Thou art the Hearing! O Thou the Compassionate God! Bestow upon me a heart which, like unto glass, may be illumined with the light of Thy love, and confer upon me a thought which may change this world into a rose-garden through the spiritual bounty. Thou art the Compassionate, the Merciful! Thou art the Great Beneficent God!

XXVI

He is the Protector and the Self-Subsistent.

I arose by Thy Favour, oh my God, and left the house depending upon Thee, and confiding my affairs unto Thee. Then send down upon me a blessing from before Thee, from the Heaven of Thy Mercy. Then make me to return to the house in safety, as Thou didst cause me to leave it in safety and steadfastness. There is no God but Thee, The Single, The One, The Knowing and the Wise.

XXVII

O thou kind God! In the utmost state of humility and submission do we entreat and supplicate at Thy threshold, seeking Thine endless confirmations and illimitable assistance.

O Thou Lord! Regenerate these souls and confer upon them a new life. Animate the spirits, inform the hearts, open the eyes and make the ears attentive. From Thine ancient treasury confer a new being and animus and from Thy pre-existent abode assist them to attain to new confirmations.

O God! Verily, the world is in need of reformation. Bestow upon it a new existence. Give it newness of thought and reveal unto it heavenly sciences. Breathe into it a fresh spirit and grant unto it a holier and higher purpose.

O God! Verily, Thou hast made this century radiant and in it Thou hast manifested Thy merciful effulgence. Thou hast effaced the darkness of superstitions and permitted the light of assurance to shine.

O God ! Grant that these servants may be acceptable at Thy threshold. Reveal a new heaven and spread out a new earth for habitation. Let a new Jerusalem descend from on high. Bestow new thoughts, new life upon mankind. Endow souls with new perceptions and confer upon them new virtues. Verily, Thou art the almighty, the powerful! Thou are the giver, the generous!

XXVIII

He is God!

O Thou Forgiving Lord! Although certain souls finished the days of their life in ignorance, were estranged and selfish, yet the Ocean of Thy Forgiveness is verily able to redeem and make free the sinners by one of its Waves. Thou redeemest whomsoever Thou willest and deprivest whomsoever Thou willest.

Shouldst Thou deal justly, we all are sinners and deserve to be deprived; but shouldst Thou observe mercy, every sinner shall be made pure and every stranger shall become a friend. Therefore forgive, pardon and grant Thy Mercy unto all. Thou art the Forgiver, the Light-Giver, and the Compassionate!

XXIX

O God, dispel all those elements which are the cause of discord and prepare for us all those things which are the cause of unity and accord.

O God! Descend upon us heavenly fragrance and change this gathering into a gathering of heaven.

Grant to us every benefit and every food. Prepare for us the food of love. Give to us the food of knowledge. Bestow upon us the food of heavenly illumination.

XXX

O my Lord, my Hope!

Praise be unto Thee, for Thou hast sent down unto us this spiritual table, supreme benefit and heavenly blessing. O our Lord! Strengthen us to partake of this heavenly food, so that its fine essence may run through the pillars of our spiritual being and that we may thereby obtain a celestial power for serving Thy Cause, promulgating Thy signs and adorning Thy vineyard with lofty trees, the fruits whereof shall be near to gather and of perfuming fragrances. Verily Thou art the Possessor of great bounty! Verily Thou are the Clement, the Merciful!

XXXI

O my Lord, my Hope! Thanks be unto Thee for these foods and benefits. O Lord! Suffer us to ascend to Thy Kingdom and to sit at the tables of thy divine world. Nourish us with the food of Thy meeting and cause us to attain to the sweetness of beholding Thy beauty, forasmuch as this is the utmost wish, the mightiest gift and the greatest bestowal. O Lord, O Lord! Make this feasible unto us. Verily Thou art the Beneficent, the Giver! Verily Thou art the Bestower, the Mighty, the Merciful.

XXXII

O God, O God, I glorify thee, O my Lord, my Hope, my beloved and the object of my life. Verily Thou knowest my humility, my evanescence, my poverty, my agitation and my shortcomings. I call on Thee with a heart overflowing with Thy love, a spirit rejoiced by the outpourings of Thy oneness, and a soul resting in Thy commemoration and praise.

O Lord, O Lord, verily these are souls who are attracted to the kingdom of Thy Holiness, hearts enkindled with the fire of Thy love and spirits soaring toward the atmosphere of Thy grace.

O Lord, O Lord, illumine our eyes with the rays of the sun of Thy reality, suffer our ears to hear, under all circumstances, the call of Thy kingdom—El-Abha.

O Lord, O Lord, make us firm in Thy Cause, humble before Thy majesty, acknowledging Thy dominion, arising in Thy service and being engaged in Thy adoration.

Verily Thou art the clement; verily Thou art the omnipotent; verily Thou art the merciful of the most merciful.

XXXIII

O God, O my Lord, I supplicate to Thee and implore in Thy presence and invoke Thee with the tongue of my conscience, my soul, my spirit, my mind, to shower down Thy merciful bestowals upon these holy souls who have gathered in this great assembly.

I beg of Thee, O my Lord, to favor them with the glances of Thy power. I entreat Thee, O my beloved, to pour upon them the rain of Thy favor from the clouds of Thy mercy. Verily these are Thy servants and Thy maidservants. Deprive them not of the sunbeams of reality; make them like waves of Thy ocean and leave them not to the darkness of themselves.

O Lord, enlighten their hearts with the Light of unity; cheer their spirits with the mystic traces of Thy knowledge; illumine their eyes with beholding Thy signs; purify their souls with the wonders of Thy majesty; inspire their consciences with the Word of Thy singleness; encircle them with Thy heavenly graces. Verily Thou art the omnipotent, the mighty. O Lord! Thou seest the hearts of humbleness before Thy dominions, the spirits attracted by Thy Holy Fragrances.

O Lord, confirm us in Thy good pleasure, assist us in Thy adoration and cause us to become worthy servants turning our faces toward the horizon of Thy singleness illumined with the rays of the sun of Thy reality.

Verily Thou art the clement, the bounteous, and verily Thou art the most merciful of the merciful!

XXXIV

Bring them together again, O Lord, by the power of Thy Covenant, and gather their dispersion by the might of Thy Promise, and unite their hearts by the dominion of Thy Love; and make them love each other so that they may sacrifice their spirits, expend their money, and give up their lives for the love of one another. O Lord, cause to descend upon them quietness and tranquillity! Shower upon them the Clouds of Thy Mercy in great abundance, and make them to adorn themselves with the attributes of the Spiritual!

O Lord, make us firm in Thy noble command and bestow upon us Thy Gifts through Thy Bounty, Grace and Munificence. Verily, Thou art the Generous, the Merciful and the Benevolent!

XXXV

O my God! O my God! We are servants who have sincerely turned our faces unto Thy grand face, severed ourselves from all else save Thee in this great day and are assembled together in this glorious meeting, of one accord and desire, and unanimous in thought to promulgate Thy Word amid Thy creatures.

O my Lord! O my Lord! Suffer us to be signs of guidance, standards of Thy manifest Religion throughout the world, servants of Thy Great Covenant—O our exalted Lord!—appearances of Thy oneness in Thy Kingdom, the El-Abha, and stars which dawn forth unto all regions.

O Lord! Make us as seas rolling with the waves of Thy great abundance, rivers flowing from the mountains of

Thy glorious Kingdom, pure fruits on the tree of Thy illustrious Cause, plants refreshed and moved by the breeze of Thy gift in Thy wonderful vineyard.

O Lord! Cause our souls to depend upon the signs of Thy Oneness, our hearts to be dilated with the bounties of Thy Singleness, so that we may become united as are ripples on a waving sea; become harmonized as are the rays which shine forth from a brilliant light; so that our thoughts, opinions and feelings become as one reality from which the spirit of accord may be diffused throughout all regions.

Verily Thou art the Beneficent, the Bestower! Verily Thou art the Giver, the Mighty, the Loving, the Merciful!

XXXVI

O kind God! Hearken to the cry of these hapless nations! O pure Lord, show Thy pity to these orphaned children! O incomparable Almighty, stop this destructive torrent! O Creator of the world and the inhabitants thereof, cause the extinction of this burning fire! O Listener to our cries, come to the rescue of the orphans! O Ideal Comforter, console the mothers whose hearts are torn and whose souls are filled with the blood of irremediable loss! O Clement and Merciful, grant the blessing of Thy grace to the weeping eyes and burning hearts of the fathers. Restore calmness to this surging tempest and change this world-encircling war into Peace and Conciliation.

Verily, Thou art the Omnipotent and the Powerful and, verily, Thou art the Seer and the Hearer!

XXXVII

O Thou kind Lord! This gathering is turning to Thee. The hearts are radiant through Thy Love. The thoughts and spirits are exhilarated through Thy glad-tidings. O God! Let this American democracy become glorious in spiritual degrees even as it has aspired to the material degrees, and render this just government victorious. Confirm this revered nation to hoist the standard of the oneness of humanity; to promulgate the Most Great Peace; to become thereby most glorious and praiseworthy among all the nations of the world. O God! This American nation is worthy of Thy favors and is deserving of Thy mercy. Make it near, dear to Thee, through Thy bounty and bestowal!

XXXVIII

O God! O Thou Who art the confirmer of every just power and equitable empire in eternal glory, the everlasting power, continuance, steadfastness, firmness and greatness! Strengthen by the abundance of Thy mercy every government which acts rightly towards its subjects and every dominion, given by Thee, that protects the poor and weak by its flags.

I ask Thee by the abundance of Thy holiness and that of Thy bounty, to assist this just government which hath stretched out the ropes of its tent to far and wide countries; the justice of which hath manifest its proofs throughout the well inhabited, cultivated and flourishing regions belonging to such government.

O God, strengthen its soldiers and flag, give authority

and influence to its word and utterance, perfect its territories and dominions, guard its reputation, make its renown widely spread, diffuse its traces and exalt its flag by Thy conquering power and wonderful might in the Kingdom of creation. Thou art the confirmer of whomsoever Thou willest. Verily, Thou art the powerful and the Almighty.

XXXIX

O Thou Almighty Lord! Strengthen all mankind that they may do according to the instructions and teachings recorded in these writings, so that wars and strifes may be eliminated from the world of man; that the roots of enmity may be destroyed and the foundations of love and affection be established; that the hearts may be filled with love and the souls be attracted; that wisdom may advance and the faces become brightened and illumined; and that reconciliation and peace appear; that the unity of the world of man may pitch its tent on the "apex of the horizons," so that peoples and parties become as one nation; that different continents become as one continent and the whole earth as one land; that the sects of antagonizing and dogmatic religions be unified; that the world of creation be adorned and all the people of the earth abide in unity and peace.

Verily, Thou art the giver, the bestower, the beholder!

XL

O my God! O my God!

These are servants who have turned to Thy Kingdom and hearkened unto Thy voice. Their hearts were dilated by Thy call, responded unto Thy summons, were attracted unto Thy beauty, acknowledged Thy proofs, believed in Thy signs, confessed Thy Oneness and arose for the service of Thy Cause and the promotion of Thy Word.

O Lord! O Lord! Make them lamps of guidance, lights glistening in the supreme apex, sparkling stars in heaven, holy angels moving on earth and thriving trees bearing delicious and fragrant fruits.

O Lord! O Lord! Purify their qualities, clarify their consciousness, cleanse their hearts and illumine their faces. Verily Thou art the Powerful, the Precious, the Protecting!

XLI

O Lord! O Lord! Bless this Spiritual Gathering, strengthen them by Thy power for the spreading of Thy divine fragrances, cause them to follow Thy will which is effective in the realities of all things, and aid them by a confirmation such as never hath preceded to any one in former centuries. For these are servants of Thy servants and Thou hast crowned them with this diadem, the most luminous gems of which will shine unto all the horizons.

Verily Thou art the Powerful, the Mighty, the Giver!

XLII

O God! O God!

Thou dost look upon us from Thine unseen Kingdom of Oneness, beholding that we have assembled in this Spiritual Meeting, believing in Thee, confident in Thy signs, firm in Thy Covenant and Testament, attracted unto Thee, set aglow with the fire of Thy love, sincere in

Thy Cause, servants in Thy vineyard, spreaders of They Religion, worshipers of Thy Countenance, humble to Thy beloved, submissive at Thy door and imploring Thee to confirm us in the service of Thy chosen ones. Support us with Thine unseen hosts, strengthen our loins in Thy servitude and make us submissive and worshiping servants, communing with Thee.

O our Lord! We are weak and Thou art the Mighty, the Powerful! We are mortals and Thou art the great life-giving Spirit! We are needy and Thou art the Powerful and Sustainer!

O our Lord! Turn our faces unto Thy divine face; feed us from Thy heavenly table by Thy godly grace; help us through the hosts of Thy supreme angels and confirm us by the holy ones of the Kingdom of Abha.

Verily Thou art the Generous, the Merciful! Thou art possessor of great bounty and verily Thou art the Clement and Gracious!

XLIII

O Thou kind Lord!

These souls are Thy friends and this gathering is longing for Thee. They are captives of the lights of Thy Beauty and ecstatic by Thy musk-scented locks. Their hearts are Thine; they are Thy poor, humble and homeless; they have severed themselves from relative and stranger and have established the relationship of unity with Thee. They have adored Thee. They were sons of earth; Thou hast made them new fruits of the Kingdom. They were plants of the desert of bereavement; Thou hast made them trees of the rose-garden of knowledge. They were silent; Thou hast made them speak. They were extinct; Thou hast lighted them. They were sterile soil; Thou hast made them the rose-garden of significances. They were the children of the world of humanity; Thou hast caused them to attain development and the maturity of the Kingdom! O kind One! Grant them shelter and security under Thy protection, preserve them from tests and trials, send them invisible help and confer upon them the doubtless bounty, O Thou kind Beloved! They are the body and Thou art the Life. The body is dependent for its life and freshness upon the Spirit—therefore they are in need of confirmation and long for the Breaths of the Holy Spirit in this new Cause!

Thou art the Able! Thou art the Giver, the Educator, the Forgiver, the Pardoner and the Light shining from the Invisible Realm!

XLIV

O my Lord! O my Lord! These are the chosen ones whose faces are illumined with the light of guidance, who found the heavenly table pleasing to their tastes, who submitted willingly to every matter which happened in the land and sought help from the hosts of the Supreme Concourse. Their feet are indeed made firm, their banners hoisted, their deeds righteous and their actions just. O Lord! Make them fragrant plants of Thy paradise, flowers of the garden of nearness, verses of Thy glorious book, words of Thy "Published Tablet" unto the people of the world and as falcons soaring on the loftiest summit. Verily Thou art the Beneficent, the Merciful, the Powerful, the Mighty, the Bestower!

XLV

O my God! O my God! Verily I am Thy humble servant

and Thy meek slave. I beseech Thee with all my heart and soul, in the middle of nights, and declare: O my Lord! O my Lord! Enlighten the eyes by the outpouring of lights; purify the souls by the fragrances of Paradise; dilate the hearts by the wafting of the breeze whereby the sorrows are dispelled, and exhilarate the spirits by the cups of the wine which is gleaming and sparkling like unto a lamp!

Then intoxicate me with the wine of Thy love, so that I may attain to success and prosperity in this dawn of Light; may speak Thy praises, call upon Thy Name, be engaged in Thy commemoration in this vast country and spacious continent and be inebriated with the pure Wine which is glowing in the excellent Cup. Then suffer me to become the sign of guidance among Thy creatures and to become a supreme example among the believers, in order that I may lead others to Thy Word, spread Thy truth, promulgate Thy knowledge and deliver Thy teachings.

Verily, Thou art the Confirmer, the Assister, the Mighty, the Powerful and the Beneficent!"

XLVI

O Thou Pure God!

Thou art the Seer and the Hearer! Thou art the Powerful and the Mighty! The fame of Thy Most Great Cause hath traveled forth and radiated from all the horizons! The believers have the utmost joy and fragrance, and the friends are attracted to the Face of that Brilliant Orb. The tongues are engaged in Thy Commemoration and the hearts are at all times dilated with the Fragrances of Thy Holiness. The faces are all turned toward Thee; the hearts are captive of Thy Abode, and the souls are athirst for the Salubrious

Water of Thy River. The call of Thy Greatest Name hath caused a mighty reverberation throughout all the kingdoms, and the Power of Thy Consummate Word hath unfurled Thy Ensign to the East and to the West! The favored ones supplicate with the utmost humility, and the righteous ones are in an attitude of soulful invocation to the Kingdom of Beauty.

O my God! Assist Thou all of them and pour upon them the showers of Thy Supreme Confirmations; so that they may become the cause of the tranquility of the world of creation; to be the servants of the human race; to become, with all their hearts and souls, the real friends of all nations; to become with the utmost joy and fragrance, the spiritual companions of the adherents of all religions; to dispel the darkness of strangeness and to spread the lights of friendship in this transitory world!

O God! Grant Thou to all of them an Asylum in Thy Neighborhood and gladden their hearts and impart to them rejoicing through Thine Incomparable Bounties! Thou are the Omnipotent and the Mighty! Thou art the Seer and the Hearer!

XLVII

O God! Thou who art kind. Verily certain souls have gathered in this meeting turning to Thee with their hearts and spirits. They are seeking the Bounty Everlasting. They are in need of Thy Mercy Infinite.

O Lord! Remove the veils from their eyes and dispel the darkness of ignorance. Confer upon them the Light of Knowledge and Wisdom. Illumine these contrite hearts with the radiance of the Sun of Reality. Make these eyes perceptive through witnessing the Lights of Thy Sovereignty. Suffer these spirits to rejoice through the great Glad Tidings and receive these souls into Thy Supreme Kingdom.

O Lord! Verily we are weak; make us mighty. We are poor; assist us from the Treasury of Thy Munificence. We are dead; resuscitate us through the breath of the Holy Spirit. We lack patience in tests and in long-suffering; permit us to attain the Lights of Oneness.

O Lord! Make this assemblage the cause of upraising the standard of the oneness of the world of humanity and confirm these souls so that they may become the promoters of international peace.

O Lord! Verily the people are veiled and in a state of contention with each other, shedding the blood and destroying the possessions of each other. Throughout the world there is war and conflict. In every direction there is strife, bloodshed and ferocity.

O Lord! Guide human souls in order that they may become loving and kind to each other; that they may enter into affiliation and serve the oneness and solidarity of humanity.

O Lord! The horizons of the world are darkened by this dissension. O God! Illumine them and through the Lights of Thy Love let the hearts become radiant. Through the blessing of Thy Bestowal resuscitate the Spirits until every soul shall perceive and act in accordance with Thy Teachings. Thou art the Almighty! Thou are the Omniscient! Thou are the Seer! O Lord be compassionate to all!

XLVIII

O my God! O my God!

This is a servant who hath ascended to the Kingdom of Thy Mercifulness; supplicated to the realm of Thy Might and Singleness; is rejoiced at the appearance of Thy

Kingdom; the effulgence of Thy lights and the spread of Thy signs. He hath believed in Thy Verses, been overtaken with the ecstasy of Thy love and with the cheer of Thy affection, until his soul craved to behold Thy Beauty—and could not or was unable to endure the grief and violence of the fire of separation, hastened unto the Supreme Friend and betook himself to Thy Threshold of Holiness at the visiting places of grandeur!

O my Lord! Suffer him to abide in a blessed abode and cause him to enter into a retreat of faithfulness and favor him to everlastingly dwell in the heavenly paradise, the precinct of meeting in the shelter of Thy great mercy!

Verily, thou art the Beneficent, the Merciful, the Powerful, the Forgiving, the Mighty, the Bestower!

XLIX

O kind Lord, verily this assemblage is longing for Thee and loving Thy beauty. Verily, these friends are set aglow with the fire of Thy love and are joyful because of Thy presence. They have turned to Thy kingdom, seeking naught but Thy good pleasure, desiring naught but to pursue Thy pathway, and seeking naught save Thy good will. Not a day passes but they are occupied with Thy commemoration and are ever ready to serve Thee.

O God, illumine these hearts. O God, make joyous these lives. O Lord, suffer these souls to attain to the superlative degree of spirituality in the world of humanity. O Lord, suffer these souls to become truly distinguished, and make them the manifestors of Thy favor and the recipients of Thy good gifts. Shine upon them with Thy radiant splendor, waft over them the breeze of Thy providence, and pour upon them the rain of bestowals from the clouds of Thy generosity. Thus these souls, like the flowers of the rose garden, shall grow in verdure and freshness, and among all mankind shall they be redolent of delightful fragrance.

O Lord, confirm them all in Thy service, and aid them in guiding others to Thee. Brighten the eyes through witnessing Thy great sign; fill the ears with harmonies through Thy melodies; and refresh the nostrils through the fragrances of Thy Kingdom. Confer upon these souls the life everlasting, gathering them all together beneath the tabernacle of the oneness of the world of humanity.

Verily, Thou art the Almighty! Verily, Thou art the Powerful! Verily, Thou art the Giver of good gifts!

SOURCES

Prayers, Tablets, Instructions and Miscellany, 1900.

Tablets of Abdu'l-Baha Abbas, 1909-1919.

The Universal Principles of the Bahai Movement, 1912.

Life and Teachings of Abbas Effendi, 1912.

Compilation of the Holy Utterances of Baha'u'llah and Abdu'l-Baha, 1918.

A Study of Bahai Prayer, 1920.

Bahai: The Spirit of the Age, 1921.

Star of the West, 1910 - 1922.

GLOSSARY

Abdu'l-Baha. "Servant of the Glory."

Aqdas. "Most Holy."

Bahai. A follower of Baha'u'llah.

Baha'u'llah. "Glory of God."

Ishraq. "Splendor."

Kheta, Khotan. Ancient kingdoms near the northwest of present China.

Mashriqu'l-Adhkar. "Dawning place of the praise and remembrance of God." A Bahai House of Worship.

Salsabil. A fountain in paradise.

Ya Baha'u'l-Abha. "O Thou Glory of the All-Glorious."